# THE ONE SON

## A Testimony of Love, Lies & Legacy

**ADRIENNE MICHELLE**

# THE ONE SON
## A TESTIMONY OF LOVE, LIES & LEGACY

ADRIENNE MICHELLE

**Copyright © 2025 by Adrienne Michelle**

All rights reserved. No part of this book may be reproduced, distributed, or transmitted in any form or by any means, including photocopying, recording, or other electronic or mechanical methods, without the prior written permission of the author, except in the case of brief quotations used in reviews or critical articles.

**Paperback ISBN:** 979-8-9941842-1-9

**Cover Design:** Adrienne Michelle

**Interior Formatting:** Adrienne Michelle

**Author Website:** amichelleproject.com

This is a work of creative nonfiction based on the author's life and recollections. Some memories have been reconstructed, condensed, or contextualized for clarity. The events portrayed are grounded in firsthand interviews conducted by the author with the individuals who lived through them.

**Privacy and Permissions Statement:**

Certain names, identities, and locations have been adjusted to protect the privacy of individuals whose lives are reflected in these pages. Any resemblance to persons living or deceased outside of those expressly identified by the author is coincidental and unintentional.

The author affirms that all individuals who appear under their real names have granted written permission for their inclusion in this memoir.

Published by Adrienne Michelle

**The One Son**

A Testimony of Love, Lies, and Legacy

For more information, visit amichelleproject.com

"Some stories stir the soul just enough for the truth to breathe."

— ADRIENNE MICHELLE

***For Mommy***
*who taught us to work hard,*
*love harder,*
*and keep faith even when the world shakes.*

***For Daddy***
*whose lessons,*
*both earned and unspoken,*
*shaped the journey.*

*And **for every member of this family***
*may the truth set you free,*
*and may love always lead you home.*

*— Adrienne Michelle*

# FOREWORD

This story is true.

Certain names, identities, and locations have been adjusted to protect the privacy of the people whose lives are on these pages.

The truth of the journey remains the same.

It is told the way it was lived, through memory, place, and the echoes of voices bold enough to participate.

Adrienne is the one who carries those voices onto the page. But she did not do it alone.

This is also her sister's story. Crystal sat beside her, asking questions, turning memories into testimony, coaxing truths from those who had long held them in silence.

What follows is no invention.

It is family; broken and beautiful, ordinary and extraordinary, scattered across time yet bound by blood and choice.

Adrienne writes it, not to excuse or condemn, but to remember. Silence was never protection. Truth is the only inheritance that lasts.

## FOREWORD

New Jersey was not the backdrop; it was the stage, the soundtrack, and the witness.

Its highways, neighborhoods, and households shaped the family and their story.

This is not myth or entertainment. It is the record of lives lived in plain sight, set to the rhythm of the Garden State.

## CHAPTER 1
# NEW JERUSALEM

People always have shit to say about Jersey.
It's the "armpit of New York," where residents eat at diners on every corner, don't pump their own gas, and drive through jughandles, curved ramps that loop drivers onto side roads so they can make left turns from the right.

The highways are misunderstood. Outsiders see traffic, tolls, and fumes. Insiders know them as veins pulsing with life. And every exit carries a story.

They dismiss the Turnpike as factories and smokestacks, though it was built for the convenience of commercial vehicles and long-distance travel.

The Garden State Parkway is treated as nothing more than a toll road with too many exits.

But for Jersey folk, the Parkway is a lifeline connecting north to south, city to shore, one generation's story to the next.

Each city carries its own rhythm; places lived, visited, or passed through. Mile markers of memory, family, and fun.

And then there's the Driscoll Bridge that spans over the Raritan River.

Crossing it feels like entering another world, the rush of fifteen lanes moving as one. It's the widest highway bridge on earth, a river of concrete and steel carrying families, dreamers, and the noise of Jersey life between the north and the south.

To the north lies the hum of New York, the promise of ambition, and late-night drives chasing possibility.

To the south, the pull of the Shore, where laughter spills from kitchens and backyards, house parties thump through basements, and reunions stretch long into the night.

Between those worlds, the Parkway rumbles like a bass line, steady and unrelenting, carrying stories, hustle, and attitude in every lane.

For this family, it's Bloomfield for roller skating at Branch Brook Park. The Oranges to party at the Peppermint Lounge. Irvington to find someone selling mixtapes or hustling plates out of a trunk. Newark to shop on Broad and Market. Red Bank for family cookouts. Eatontown for shopping runs at the Monmouth Mall. Long Branch for a stroll on the boardwalk. Neptune for the Premium Outlets. Asbury Park for rides that never lasted long enough.

Jersey made icons and owned its legends. No last names required.

Meryl from Summit. Jack from Neptune. Carli from Delran. Carl from Willingboro. And long before them, Paul as in Robeson from Princeton.

Newark did its part, shaping greats like Joe, Shaquille, Michael B., and Cory, who carried "Brick City" all the way to Washington, DC, as the first Black Senator.

The Jersey soundtrack was unmatched.

Count Basie from Red Bank. Bruce from Long Branch. Frank from Hoboken. Whitney from Newark. Jon from Sayreville. Kool & the Gang from Jersey City. And Melba, Newark raised, Montclair State College trained.

Their voices carried everywhere, from arenas to car radios, from summers on the boardwalk to basement parties.

Music exploded from turntables and released hip hop energy that made history.

The Sugarhill Gang out of Englewood gave the world *Rapper's Delight*.

Newark showed up again with Queen Latifah, calling for *U.N.I.T.Y.* and then carrying that same spirit into *Living Single*, where her voice opened every episode like a manifesto, celebrating independence, sisterhood, and a '90s world where women stood tall, leaned on each other, and moved freely through life together.

Naughty by Nature, with Treach, Vin Rock, and DJ Kay Gee, made East Orange feel like the center of the hip hop universe, with *O.P.P.* and *Hip-Hop Hooray* turning block parties into national anthems and giving the city a sound all its own.

Even the family tree carries echoes of that beat. Adrienne's grandmother married Vin Rock's father, tying their family by marriage to the very voices calling out of East Orange.

The music lived in the air and in the bloodlines, woven into Sunday dinners and family gossip.

Lauryn Hill of South Orange turned their childhood into testimony.

In *Every Ghetto, Every City*, she did not just remember the past; she resurrected it. The Saturdays, the neighborhood rituals, the way music floated through open windows in the summer heat. She caught it all and pressed it into a sound that felt like home for anyone raised on Jersey pavement. Her song felt like standing in your own childhood again, seeing the world the way you first learned it.

Drill teams took over Munn Street back then. Boots cracked against the asphalt, snare drums bouncing off the bricks, the kind of rhythm that settled in your chest and stayed there long after the parade passed.

Central Avenue moved differently. Beauty salons hummed with gossip and hair spray, record shops lived off the heartbeat of bass lines, and bars let their music spill onto sidewalks as if the street itself needed a soundtrack.

Frelinghuysen Avenue had its own rules. On Friday nights the bomb leathers came out, fades sharp enough to catch the streetlight, sneakers clean like you cared about how you walked into a room.

But that strip sold more than jackets, beef patties, and coco bread. It sold caution. It taught you how to clock the shadows, how to keep your voice steady, how to survive without announcing your fear.

Her cousin George learned that lesson when someone snatched his leather bomber, a Jersey baptism no one volunteered for, but everybody understood.

Aunt Tee always said, "Put your money in different places when you go shopping, never all in one pocket."

It sounded simple, almost funny, but it was really training, a quiet guide for walking through a world that does not always play fair.

Lauryn caught that truth in her music. She named it New Jerusalem; a place built on equal parts grit and grace.

For kids like them, every block was a classroom. Every sound taught rhythm. Every corner taught survival. Every street taught pride.

Long before anyone put Jersey on a map, they knew it was already a kingdom carved into concrete, memory, and heartbeat.

Jersey gave laughter. Comedians like Flip Wilson, Sommore, Michelle Buteau, and Tisha Campbell, whose journey from Newark Arts High School to living rooms everywhere made Gina on *Martin* unforgettable.

Survival had its weight, but celebration always found a stage.

In the 1980s and 1990s, the Peppermint Lounge in East Orange was comedy's proving ground.

Before Chris Rock and Steve Harvey sold out arenas, they stood under those lights.

Bill Bellamy, Newark's own, hosted nights where the crowd was part ruthless, part loyal. The Peppermint didn't hand out respect; you earned it, joke by joke, with hecklers daring you to fail and applause daring you to keep going.

It wasn't only for stars. The Peppermint belonged to locals who carried the same grit and spirit that pulsed through Jersey streets, working by day, coming alive at night, filling the club with smoke, laughter, and the charge of possibility.

Adrienne knew that charge well. After classes at Montclair State, she worked late nights at The Peppermint as a waitress, weaving through tables heavy with cocktails and noise.

It was survival and tuition money, but also a front-row seat to Jersey's heartbeat. She heard the jokes before they were famous, felt the rhythm of voices rising and falling like a second language.

On tired mornings, when the hustle of the night spilled into the discipline of the day, she carried that rhythm into class.

There, her professor, Dr. Saundra, pushed her to confront the psychology of the Black experience and revealed that Black thought was never just a critique. It was a blueprint for future development, a call to advance a discipline that tells the truth about a people who always deserved more than the theories built to contain them.

One night, she and her friends Alledine, Monique, Ruelda

and Valerie took the Peppermint stage themselves to mark their graduation from Montclair State. They called it "Five Women with a Degree."

The Lounge was filled wall to wall, not because anyone was chasing fame but because achievement demanded celebration. Degrees in their hands, courage in their voices, they stood where legends had stood and claimed their moment.

Celebration did not end at the podium. It simply changed locations, trading velvet ropes for familiar roads and the promise of home.

Off an exit leading to the Shore Points, she knew she was almost home.

Once she came off the Garden State Parkway, family waited; grills smoking, cards slapping on folding tables, impromptu fashion shows turning living rooms into runways.

Voices rose and tangled in the humid air, stretching long into the night.

But rhythms shift.

Not every gathering ended in joy.

The same Parkway that led home also taught consequences. The kitchens went quiet with truth. The basements became places to cry in the dark. Music became anthems that carried the pain.

At one of the gatherings, a revelation crashed through the good time, like a hit and run accident; shattering trust, breaking bonds, leaving everyone dazed.

## CHAPTER 2
# THE CRASH

It was like riding in the back seat on a bright sunny afternoon.

Windows down. Warm breeze. New Edition on the radio. Everything felt beautiful and safe.

Then, out of nowhere, another car blew through the intersection.

Metal against metal. Impact unavoidable.

That's how truth hit the family: sudden, violent, without warning.

They weren't the target, just in the way. And in an instant, they were the casualties.

At fifty miles per hour, the world doesn't stop gently. Everyone in the back seat flies through the front window.

The glass. The metal. The pain.

A sunny day turns into twisted wreckage.

Blood on the pavement. Silence where there had been music.

For Adrienne when the truth came crashing in, nothing felt safe again.

She was fourteen, standing in the kitchen, when the words were dropped so casually as if they meant nothing.

She doesn't even remember who said them, probably a cousin who overheard the adults talking.

What she does remember is the sound of it, sharp and final.

"She's your father's child."

The words struck on impact. No story. No explanation. No comfort.

Just words that shattered everything she thought she knew.

Adrienne left the kitchen, walked into the small bathroom, and closed the door. The mirror was fogged, the walls pressing in close, her chest rising too fast. It felt like she was outside her own body, confused and watching herself break.

"Could it really be true that her cousin was her sister?"

The pain was sharp, though no one else seemed to notice. She was left bleeding, expected to carry the wounds in silence.

When the dust settled, Adrienne wasn't the only one sprawled across the wreckage. Her brothers Barry Jr. and Carlos, their cousin Sonny, and their mother Sandra were there too, each one broken in the street.

On this day, inside their home where good times always lived, the truth hit like a carjacking, seizing their lives without warning.

No one explained. No one consoled. No one accepted responsibility.

There they were, the entire family, left bleeding in the street while the perpetrators drove away and the eyewitnesses stood by in silence.

Who were the culprits behind this hit and run?

Their father, Barry, sat in the passenger seat, their aunt, Janice, in the back, both of their eyes fixed straight ahead, refusing to glance in the rearview mirror. His other sisters stood on the side of the road, as witnesses who would not testify.

And Dorothy, his mother, their grandmother. She was behind the wheel, pressing the gas.

Dorothy was the architect of the deception, the driver of the collision. She steered the lie, demanded silence, and swore everyone to secrecy to protect her One Son, her prized possession, the child she held closest to her heart.

When he faltered, it was his life she wanted to save. He was the one she rushed to the hospital. And if keeping him alive meant silencing the truth, burying the shame, or breaking the rest of them in the process, so be it.

Barry was living on the life support his mother Dorothy provided.

What no one realized was that he had been hooked up to that support for years. And with this revelation, the plug had finally been pulled.

## CHAPTER 3
# THE ONE SON

The wreckage lay scattered and no one dared gather it. The silence was its own testimony.

To understand why the crash happened, why trust shattered, why silence ruled, you had to trace it back to the driver.

Barry was always a loner. Not lonely, just alone in how he moved through the world. He learned early that silence was protection and solitude was strategy.

"Do your dirt alone," he told himself, "So there are no witnesses, no one to testify, no one to prove what really happened, no one to hold you accountable."

To understand him, to understand how his view of life bent the way it did, you had to start with the tether: a son who never cut the cord from his mother.

Dorothy was still a child when she became a mother. She was fourteen and Karl was eighteen when Francis was born, everyone called her Franny. Too young to understand what motherhood required, Dorothy was still trying to grow up herself.

Four years after Franny, at eighteen, Dorothy gave birth to Barry. From the moment she held him, something shifted. Her arms lingered longer, her gaze softer. He became her reason, her reflection, the heartbeat that steadied her.

Later came Barbara, whom the family called Dina. Barry was never certain if Dina's father was Karl or another man; by the time she was born, Dorothy and Karl were separated, and someone else had already entered the picture. Still, Karl claimed her, and she bore his last name.

When Barry was nine or ten, Dorothy married Edward. Their marriage marked a turning point for Franny, Barry and Dina, the moment when abuse entered the home like an uninvited guest.

Edward's temper infected everything. He beat Dorothy so often that men on the block would take justice into their own hands, jumping him whenever she had bruises. Dorothy wasn't the only one who felt his rage. Barry did too. The house became a place of fear, its walls shrinking smaller each day.

Through it all, Franny made life bearable. She was Barry's closest ally, the one who could lift the weight from his shoulders with a laugh or a glance.

So, when Dorothy kicked Franny out, the void was immediate. She went to live with their grandmother Eva, who lived just behind them. Barry never knew the full story, but he suspected Edward had something to do with it. Whatever the reason, Franny not living there left him without his strongest support. The house grew colder.

Among Adrienne's fondest memories of Franny was the day she took her and her cousins to a double feature of Sparkle and Fame, both starring Irene Cara. Adrienne couldn't carry a tune, but that afternoon etched something lasting. She fell in love with song and dance as a language of expression, a way to feel joy and tell stories.

Dorothy and Edward had two girls: Elaine, whom the family called Laney, and Janice, the baby.

Born into a house of anger, they knew no other life. Their harshness made its own kind of sense; after all, what's in the blood don't rot.

Whether their cruelty came from what they witnessed or what they endured, they passed it along like a family heirloom, reshaped but never gone.

Adrienne called Laney, Evillene, the Wicked Witch of the West, and Janice, Evvamean, the Wicked Witch of the East.

It made sense.

Laney carried the same loud, intimidating flair as Evillene from The Wiz, a woman who thrived on drama, demanded control, and filled any room long before she stepped into it. She barked orders with confidence and expected everyone to fall in line.

Janice had volume too, but hers came with a harder edge. She did not glide. She stormed. She entered a room like a warning, heavy and unavoidable, and she was just mean. She did not hide her judgment, and she did not cushion her words. People hurried because Janice watched everything and she used what she saw. Her power was loud, sharp, and meant to sting.

To outsiders, both women looked gentle, even motherly. Beneath that softness they moved like trained witches, disguising manipulation as care and control as protection.

Dorothy stood above them as the original source of their power. She was the mother of witches, the true sorceress who created them. Her authority did not need volume. People adjusted themselves when she entered, not out of fear but out of instinct. She taught her daughters that softness invited danger and vulnerability invited loss.

Laney inherited her dramatic flair and thunderous presence. Janice took up her force, her judgment, and her ability to strike without hesitation.

Together they reflected the sorceress and the storm she released into the world.

Dorothy's control went far beyond anything she said. She knew how to turn devotion into duty and loyalty into obligation. Barry became an extension of her power, carrying out her authority through his unquestioning obedience.

Once, when Dina was eleven or twelve, Dorothy accused her of talking to a boy from Detroit. Dina denied it, but Dorothy ordered Barry to punish her. He obeyed. In that moment, he stopped being a brother and became her enforcer. Dorothy didn't care how the punishment scarred Dina. Abuse was her language, and she spoke it fluently.

Sandra, Barry's high school sweetheart, came over afterward and found Dina crying. She gathered her in her arms, cradling her against the weight of what happened. In Sandra's embrace, Dina saw compassion where cruelty ruled. She caught a glimpse of what love could look like inside a house that rarely offered any.

Dina never forgot it.

From that day forward, she admired Sandra's mix of gentleness and strength, holding onto the memory of the first person in that home who treated her with real care. Sandra continued to look after Dina over the years, and Dina came to see her as a big sister.

Whether she confronted Barry is unknown, but knowing Sandra, she made her stance clear: he was never to raise a hand to her, or they were done.

As for Dorothy, he was her everything, her prized possession, the center of her world. The girls knew he was her favorite, and she didn't try to hide it.

To be the One Son was never a matter of birth order. It was

a mantle built from absence, need, and history. Dorothy clung to Barry as her anchor, and he clung to her in return. They mirrored each other; Dorothy holding fast to what she knew, Barry bound to her as if growing free meant losing himself.

The grandchildren called Dorothy "Nonny," a name meant to show affection.

Adrienne never embraced it. She felt a distance she could not cross and never claimed Dorothy as her own grandmother. In Adrienne's heart, there was only one grandmother, her mother's mother, Mary, who everyone called Nanna.

Barry was the uncle the other children looked to as the man of the family in a world where most fathers were gone, dead, or absent.

That role carried weight. Admiration turned to expectation, and expectation to obligation.

To the children in the family, he was the authority. He never had to spank anyone; his voice and stare were enough. Everyone except Adrienne was afraid of him. When he entered a room, the kids straightened up and went quiet. His presence alone demanded order.

The ugliness of his childhood stood in contrast to his appearance. Where the past was marked by pain and scarcity, the man who emerged was striking; six feet tall, light skinned, bow legged, with a deep, velvety voice like Barry White's. He was magnetic, especially to Black women. Even in old age, the aura remained.

He was an avid reader, often juggling several thick novels at once, most on politics and history. He stayed current with the news, always aware of the world beyond his own.

Against the shadow of his childhood, he carried himself with a calm that told a different story.

## CHAPTER 4
# BAD MAMA JAMA

And then there was Sandra, everything Barry's quiet was not. Where he moved in measured silence, she brought color, energy, and life.

She was a Bad Mama Jama, her presence pure poetry in motion, her style impossible to miss.

She didn't need anyone to tell her she was sexy. She knew it. She didn't need anyone to tell her she was smart.

She knew that too. Funny? She knew it. Crazy? She knew it.

She marched to the beat of her own drum no matter what song was playing. The party started when she walked in and ended when she turned on the lights.

It was no wonder Barry was drawn to her. Where Barry was bound, she was free.

Newark, New Jersey was where it all started. Sandra, the daughter of Mary and George, was born into a city of rhythm, resilience, and rising dreams.

Mary's life began in tragedy. Her mother died when she was only six days old, and her father followed six months later under mysterious circumstances the family said was a snake bite.

Raised in Atlanta, Georgia by her grandmother and her grandmother's sisters, Big Baby and Little Baby, Mary grew up in a house where cousins were treated as siblings and family was everything. Even as a girl she carried defiance in her bones, standing on the curb to hurl rocks at the Ku Klux Klan as they marched through the streets of Atlanta.

George's path was marked by flight and fire. A refugee from Florida, he fled after being cast out for beating up a white man. Before that, he had been tricked into marriage by a girl who claimed she was pregnant; her lie exposed when no child appeared. He carried both anger and charm, the kind of man who knew how to fight and how to keep moving. His troubles lingered, and excessive drinking became his way of dulling the weight.

Together, Mary and George ran a household that balanced structure with survival. Mary brought the discipline of Atlanta's crowded rooms, where family was in abundance and the unyielding strength that came from hardship. George carried the restless energy of a man who had lived by his fists and his wit, a presence both magnetic and unpredictable.

Their household was equal parts discipline and chaos, survival and strategy.

Six children filled the rooms, each with their own beat: Gwendolyn, the oldest, wild and uncontainable; Mary often said every word out of her mouth was probably a lie.

Patricia, heaven-sent, devoted to the Lord, her Savior, her truth and her light.

Beverly, the educated one, serious about her own learning and just as serious about educating everyone around her.

George, nicknamed Porgie after the nursery rhyme

"Georgie Porgie, Pudding and Pie," the jokester, always chasing fun, a drink in reach, and laughter close by.

John, the youngest, an out-of-the-box thinker, drawn to art and the finer things in life.

Space was tight. Gwen and Pat shared a room. Sandra and Beverly, just eleven months apart, shared a room. George and John shared a room.

Sandra and her sisters communicated in Pig Latin, a language that kept its secrets in plain sight.

Adrienne once thought it was some kind of Black secret language, one she wanted badly to understand but never quite mastered.

Sandra and her sisters spoke it fast and fluid, flipping sounds in real time while the meaning stayed perfectly intact. Consonants shifted, endings picked up ay or way, syllables rearranged so quickly that the message vanished for anyone not trained to hear it.

They could hold an entire adult conversation right in front of the children, never lowering their voices and never leaving the room. To outsiders it sounded playful, even silly. To them it was precise and efficient.

Pig Latin wasn't unique to them.

It was a common English word game, popular with children across cultures as a simple code for playful, covert communication. It dated back to the nineteenth century and became widely recognizable through American movies and television in the early twentieth.

Still, Adrienne did not recall ever hearing white people speak it at all.

In Sandra's house, it was spoken openly and at full speed.

For Black folk, Pig Latin was often compared to something older and far more deliberate. Tutnese, sometimes called Tut or the King Tut language, had been developed generations earlier by enslaved African Americans as a complex coded system used to communicate privately and to secretly learn to read. It was not a game but a safeguard, built word by word to protect knowledge and survival.

Pig Latin did not carry that history, but in Sandra's family it served a similar function. It created distance. It controlled access. It decided who was in and who was not.

What baffled Adrienne was how good Sandra was at it, considering she was notorious for misspelling words.

What she did not understand then was that Pig Latin rewards a certain kind of mind. You must hear words before you see them.

Speaking Pig Latin is an auditory and verbal skill, not a written one. It lives in sound and instinct rather than spelling or rules.

Sandra had a beautiful mind. She always knew what to say and how to say it, and even when others in the room missed the meaning, the person she was speaking to understood her perfectly.

Mary always said Sandra was the only one of her six children who never got in trouble and never got a spanking. Not because she was perfect. She just learned early, don't talk back, do what you're told, and cover your tracks.

When others tried to be slick, she'd laugh and remind them, "You can't outslick a slickster."

Sandra also had an eye for fashion and a sense of style that showed early. Every outfit she touched carried her signature. It was a light entirely her own. It was a gift.

Compared to Barry's childhood, Sandra's life was more Huxtable than harsh.

She graduated from Barringer High School in 1966, one of the oldest public high schools in the country. At Barringer, she stood out for her confidence and unmistakable style, carrying herself with the same assurance she would later take wherever she went.

Barringer was also where she met Barry, her high school sweetheart.

It was Barry's cousin's girlfriend who introduced him to Sandra. She thought they'd make a good match, Barry with his quiet confidence, Sandra with her poise.

Sandra was drawn to something steady and mysterious in him. Barry liked that she was sharp, focused, and unafraid to speak her mind.

They came from different worlds. She was raised on discipline and expectation; he was raised on survival.

Given those differences, it was surprising Mary and George allowed them to see each other.

Knowing Sandra, she probably never asked.

They lived in the Archbishop Thomas Walsh Housing Projects, twelve brick buildings lined up along McCarter Highway, pressed close to the polluted Passaic River. The endless red-brick high-rises stacked against the skyline looked like giant matchboxes piled one on top of the other, the image that gave Newark its name: Brick City.

Back then, the Projects didn't automatically mean poverty. Many families were working-class, two-parent households. Inside those walls, the Scotts were not defined by lack but by presence, crowded kitchens, cousins and friends in and out, voices overlapping, stories spilling late into the night.

Dating in the Walsh Projects had its own tempo, and with three older girls seeing boys, it became part of the building's routine. Gwen with George, Pat with Milton, and Sandra with Barry; each pairing had their place, meeting on different floors.

No matter where they were, the rule was clear: all three girls had to be back in their apartment by curfew. Mary's sharp eyes kept watch, and even if she wasn't looking, the neighbors were.

After graduation, Sandra went to work in bridal shops. Her style and precision showed in every garment she constructed. Fashion lived in her bones, and she carried it with confidence.

That drive carried her to FIT, the Fashion Institute of Technology in New York.

For a Black girl in the late 1960s, that was rare. The fashion world then didn't look like her. White models. White designers. White editors. To walk through those doors, her work had to be undeniable.

At FIT, Sandra threw herself into the grind, sketching designs late into the night, cutting and sewing fabric until her fingertips were sore, pressing seams with precision. She studied textiles, construction, and draping, but what set her apart was vision. She could see shape and style before the cloth even touched the form.

New York itself was a classroom. Walking through the Garment District, she studied shop windows and mannequins, watching how trends were set and sold. She carried notebooks, jotting details others missed, the line of a collar, the swing of a hem, the way a bold color drew every eye in the room.

She was not alone. Future legends filled those same classrooms. Arthur McGee broke barriers on Seventh Avenue. Jon Haggins carved out international success. Bethann Hardison moved from design to modeling to activism, shaping the industry from every angle. Ademola Olugebefola's art rose alongside the Black Arts Movement.

Others who would redefine fashion passed through those halls as well. Norma Kamali reinvented women's wear. Calvin Klein studied at FIT before launching a global empire. And years later, Laverne Cox carried the school's influence into acting, advocacy, and the red carpet.

To stand among those names proved Sandra belonged.

## CHAPTER 5
# WAR, WHAT IS IT GOOD FOR?

B arry was never built for confinement. Not the classroom. Not the house. Not the rules.

At Barringer High, he was a smooth talker with a presence that drew attention even when he said little. He didn't joke much or show off. He simply didn't take school seriously. He cut class, drifted through hallways, and lived like the rules didn't apply to him.

Barringer finally expelled him for truancy. In those days, skipping school in New Jersey wasn't just rebellion. It was a crime. Truancy officers had full police power and could arrest any student found out of class without cause.

Barry learned that the hard way. After one arrest too many, he found himself behind bars. Edward refused to bail him out. Not to teach him a lesson, but because he was just mean. Barry spent two weeks locked up while his mother tried to intervene and failed. When he finally stood before a judge, he was given a choice: return to jail or join the military.

In the 1960s, some judges gave men a choice between jail or the military. For many, it wasn't much of a choice at all. The system was drawn in black and white, stacked against Black men and the poor, pushing them into uniforms while white men found ways out through college or connections. Poor Black boys went to war while privileged white ones stayed home.

Draft boards didn't look like the communities they served, and the burden fell on those who had the least. It became another kind of sentence, another way America punished and used its own, sending them to fight for freedoms they still couldn't claim when they returned.

But for Barry, the ultimatum was a lifeline. It wasn't escape from jail; it was escape from the abuse at home.

The following week, he enlisted.

The Army saved his life.

It gave him discipline, a GED, a career, and eventually a college degree. It gave him order, purpose, and boundaries no one at home had enforced.

In Basic and Advanced Individual Training, days ran like clockwork, a 9-to-5 of drills, sweat, and barked orders. For a young man who had known only chaos, that structure felt almost merciful.

After training with the 1st Cavalry Division, he shipped out to Vietnam.

A high school dropout, abused by his stepfather, and his mother's prized possession, he now found himself living in a foreign land.

He had never been beyond the New Jersey state line, let alone out of the country, but the Army didn't care about readiness. It cared about numbers. Vietnam was already burning, and America kept feeding it their sons.

The news called it a conflict. The streets called it a death sentence. For young Black men, it was both. By 1965, they made up nearly a third of the Army's ground combat troops, though they were only twelve percent of the U.S. population. The math was merciless. Black boys were dying faster than anyone wanted to count.

Loneliness sat heavy at night, and his mother's voice was the one he heard when the noise quieted.

Even in uniform, Barry was still Dorothy's boy. He wrote her often, telling her how much he missed his momma. A man of contradictions, his pen revealed a softer truth. Beneath the hardness, his handwriting was precise, disciplined, almost delicate. The lines were even, the spacing exact, the letters upright and calm. Each stroke carried quiet beauty, a controlled grace that hinted at the tenderness he rarely showed.

While others noticed the sternness, the deep voice, the striking good looks, his handwriting showed a different kind of strength, measured, thoughtful, and controlled. Sometimes his penmanship even eclipsed the words themselves.

Barry's unit worked communications, stationed beneath a steep mountain that anchored the division's network. The jungle was wet, heavy, and loud. Everything smelled like metal and smoke.

For young African American soldiers, the war came with a second battle: racism. They fought beside white men who still refused to eat with them, salute them, or call them by name. News of civil-rights marches came faintly over Armed Forces Radio, and they wondered how freedom could be defended abroad while denied at home.

He found comfort in brotherhood, card games, makeshift barbershops, Motown spinning on battered tape decks. Laughter in short supply became a form of resistance.

Once, a package arrived from home, a fully cooked chicken mailed by his aunt. By the time it reached him, it was green, spoiled, and stinking. He laughed anyway. Even rotten, it smelled like care. It was love wrapped in foil and faith that he was still close enough to feed.

Moments like that broke the heaviness of distance, reminding him that even in the middle of war, love had a way of finding him, no matter how spoiled or strange its delivery.

Then one night, the mountain erupted. The Viet Cong hit hard, lighting up the sky in red and orange. The base shook. Barry was only seventeen, barely out of boyhood, thrown into a war that demanded a man's steadiness long before he had time to grow into it.

In the chaos, a sergeant who had not been issued his rifle asked if Barry could handle his weapon. Barry said yes. The man reached for it anyway. Barry stayed calm, steady in a way his age should not have allowed. If he tried to take it, they would find out just how well he could use it.

The sergeant backed off.

Barry never forgot that moment, the panic, the restraint, the razor-thin distance between fear and control. He saw the Viet Cong only once, but for a seventeen-year-old far from home, once was enough.

When his tour ended, he came home changed.

Barry returned to Newark in uniform: leaner, sharper, transformed in posture and presence. The boy who once drifted through hallways now moved like a man who had seen the edge and come back from it. The uniform did what years of lectures never could. It demanded respect.

Neighbors stared. Women noticed.

Even the men who once dismissed him now nodded with quiet acknowledgment. He carried himself differently. Shoulders back. Voice low. Eyes older.

Back in America, the mood shifted. Protests filled the streets. Mothers wept on live television.

Artists turned anguish into anthems. Edwin Starr

demanded answers in a voice that felt like a rallying cry, and Marvin Gaye urged the nation to look at itself with honesty. Those songs were more than hits. They were truth set to rhythm, the sound of a country losing faith in its own decisions.

Barry did not say much about the war, but the silence wrapped around him like another uniform.

We can only imagine what happened when Sandra saw him again. Maybe it was during a school break, or maybe he appeared in New York without warning while she was away studying.

Perhaps the sun caught the shine of his brass, or maybe it was the shift in his walk that made her pause.

The boy who once cut class and wasted hours was gone. In his place stood a man with a tapered haircut, a pressed uniform, and boots that clicked with purpose. He smiled, and in that moment, she might have forgotten every warning her parents ever offered.

Or maybe she was simply stunned, the way a great romance scene stops time. When they stood together, the pull between them was unmistakable, effortless and electric, the kind of chemistry that spoke for itself.

## CHAPTER 6
# AIN'T NOTHING LIKE THE REAL THING

After two years at FIT, Sandra faced a choice. The city pulled her forward with late nights of sketches and fabric, professors who recognized her eye, and the thrill of being part of something larger than herself.

Yet Newark pulled her back. Barry had returned from Vietnam, grateful Sandra had waited for him, determined now to make her his wife. Their bond, steady since high school, carried the weight of distance, survival, and reunion. For Barry, love became a compass. For Sandra, it moved through her like a needle through fabric.

When he asked Sandra to marry him, she knew that meant leaving school, leaving the life she'd planned, and stepping into a future built on both love and uncertainty.

In the end, love won. Sandra left FIT to marry Barry.

On April 28, 1968, in Newark, New Jersey, they began their life together. Just nineteen and twenty-one, they were a young power couple before the world had a name for it. Sandra used her talent to craft her wedding gown, sewing every bead by hand for an elegance that stood the test of time.

Barry found more than a wife in Sandra; he found family. His own relationship with his father was distant, and his stepfather carried his disdain. But with Sandra's parents, he felt something different. He called them affectionately Momma and Poppa Scott.

He formed a bond, especially with Poppa Scott, riding shotgun with him to and from the local bars, listening, venting, and unloading about his relationship with Sandra. Barry felt a connection that steadied him, one that made him feel less like an outsider and more like he belonged.

They honeymooned in Atlantic City, the glittering crown of the Jersey Shore. In 1968, it was still the East Coast's playground, a stretch of glamour that shimmered with music, motion, and a restless kind of energy.

The boardwalk glowed with neon marquees; the smell of caramel corn and sea breeze tangled in the air. Steel Pier still drew crowds for high-diving acts and live performances, while the rolling waves whispered just beyond the laughter and buzz of arcade bells.

For Black couples like Barry and Sandra, Atlantic City held its own corner of freedom. Segregation lingered quietly, but on the Northside, life pulsed with its own energy. Chicken Bone Beach, just off Missouri Avenue, was their safe space, a strip of sand claimed by Black families since the 1930s.

The air buzzed with music and laughter, the smell of suntan oil and barbecue mingling as children splashed in the surf. Everyone dressed sharp even at the shore, with pressed shorts, bold prints, sunglasses, and straw hats tilted just right. It was a place where they could be seen, beautiful, and unbothered.

At night, the scene shifted to Kentucky Avenue, where the heartbeat of the city never stopped. Club Harlem was the crown jewel. Its stage had seen Count Basie, Sarah Vaughan, and Sammy Davis Jr.

Between the late-night jazz sets and early morning soul sessions, the club blurred the line between night and day. Barry loved the horns, the rhythm, the control beneath the chaos. Sandra loved the gowns, the sequins, the swing of it all, the way women floated to the floor in elegance and men in tailored suits commanded space without saying a word.

They fit right in. Sandra's style turned heads; tailored, feminine, confident. Barry, with his smooth frame and quiet composure, carried himself like someone who had seen the world and come back sharper for it. Together, they looked like they belonged to that golden hour between modesty and magic.

They spent their days walking the boardwalk, sharing bags of taffy from Fralinger's and fresh seafood from the docks. In the evenings, they'd drift from small jazz lounges to the bigger rooms where the music pulsed until dawn.

Somewhere between the lights and the laughter, a Marvin Gaye and Tammi Terrell classic floated through the room, its melody rising above the crowd. For Barry, that song was Sandra. For Sandra, it was Barry. They were young, Black, and in love in a time that did not always make room for either.

They ate fried clams wrapped in paper, leaned against the railing to watch the moon ripple across the water, and danced barefoot in their hotel room when the night grew quiet. The hotel had a heart-shaped tub, and they splashed water everywhere, laughing so hard their voices carried down the hall.

The lights, the pulse of jazz and Motown, and the ocean breeze witnessed their first days as husband and wife. On that stretch of boardwalk, with the world still uncertain and the nation still aching from war, Barry and Sandra found a moment of peace that belonged entirely to them.

ADRIENNE MICHELLE

The Shore carried the beginning of their marriage. For them, the kind of love they had could never be imitated, no matter how many songs tried to describe it.

All good things must come to an end.

The promenade and late-night jazz yielded to formations, duty rosters, and base routines.

## CHAPTER 7
# KILLEEN

Their married life began in uniform and on the move. After the wedding, the Army sent Barry to Fort Hood, now Fort Cavazos, with the 3rd Armored Corps. The Corps served as a major training and deployment hub for troops bound for Vietnam. They trained and sent more than 100,000 personnel overseas, including two Field Force headquarters, while also processing thousands returning from service.

As the military was preparing for war on the post, African Americans prepared for survival off post.

Fort Hood is in Killeen, Texas. Black folks would say Killeen was an acronym for "Kill Each and Every Nigga," a warning for Black people. Racism there ran deep. Not a joke or exaggeration, but a threat. It was a sundown town. Black residents knew not to be caught on the streets after dark.

The rule was unwritten but understood. Don't be in the wrong neighborhood. Don't linger too long. Don't draw attention. Military uniforms didn't shield you. Marriage licenses didn't protect you. Respectability didn't buy safety. The menace hung over the streets, making every nightfall a reminder of who held power and who was expected to disappear when darkness fell.

Just a year earlier, in the summer of 1967, Newark had erupted after rumors spread that police had killed a Black cab driver. Though the driver survived, badly beaten, the city burned for days. Twenty-six people were killed, hundreds injured, and whole blocks left scarred, damage Newark has yet to fully recover from.

Now, barely a year later, Barry and Sandra found themselves in Killeen, Texas, trading one kind of fire for another. Newark's rage was loud, with smoke and sirens filling the streets. Killeen's racism was quiet but constant, the kind that struck at nightfall and whispered every unspoken rule of the South.

They had grown up in the racism of the North and thought they knew its edges. What they found in Texas was a different kind of menace. It didn't always explode in riots or make headlines. It crept into daily life, equally dangerous, equally life-threatening; a reminder that hate could change form but not intent.

That same year, Fort Hood became the site of a historic protest. On August 23, 1968, 60 Black soldiers held a peaceful sit-in against orders to deploy to Chicago for riot control during the Democratic National Convention, viewing it as being used against their own people amid the Civil Rights Movement. After negotiations, the 43 soldiers who refused to comply were jailed, court-martialed, and sentenced to hard labor. The "Fort Hood 43" protest remains one of the largest acts of dissent in U.S. military history.

From Newark's uprising in 1967 to Fort Hood in 1968, the threat was the same.

After sixteen months of marriage, Barry and Sandra

welcomed their first child, Adrienne. She was born on August 9, 1969, in Killeen at 1:13 a.m., just hours before the Manson murders in Los Angeles, California.

Chaos and creation. Death and birth.

The coincidence cast a shadow, evil spilling into the headlines at the very moment new life entered their family, a foreshadowing of how darkness would one day shape their own story. Even then, California was written into Adrienne's timeline, a connection that would surface later in ways no one could have predicted.

Adrienne's name came not from Barry or from Sandra but from Barry's mother Dorothy.

Even as a married man, Barry, the One Son, remained tethered to his mother, her influence shaping decisions that should have belonged to him and Sandra alone. Dorothy was a powerful presence, strong-willed and unyielding, and Barry was still caught in her orbit. It was Dorothy who decided what his firstborn would be called, imprinting her authority onto Adrienne before the child could even open her eyes.

Dorothy may have thought she was shaping the child's destiny by naming her Adrienne, "Dark One." But the future would prove otherwise. The name carried mystery, depth, and duality.

True to it, Adrienne embodied traits that marked her from the start: intellectually curious and introspective, with a restless creativity that spilled out in observations and questions too big for her age.

She longed for harmony, instinctively nurturing connections and reading emotions around her with ease. Adaptable and engaging, she could be bold in one moment and shy in the next, her sensitivity both a strength and a burden.

That sensitivity often left her vulnerable, quick to self-doubt, yet it also deepened her empathy, making her a child who could bend under pressure but never break.

If Sandra resented Dorothy's control, she did not show it. Holding her tongue was not a weakness. It was strategy. Sandra had grown up knowing which battles to fight and which to let pass. She was skilled at getting her way without revealing her hand. Just as she had avoided trouble as a girl by moving quietly in the background, she now held her silence as a wife, watching, calculating, and waiting.

What Dorothy did not account for was the tether between Barry and his firstborn. Adrienne was not only the One Son's child; she was his soft spot. That bond became her power, giving her strength enough to challenge her grandmother's authority and, in time, compete for the first position in Barry's life, a place Dorothy had long claimed for herself.

## CHAPTER 8
# CHOCOLATE CITY

Leaving behind the hostility of Killeen, Barry and Sandra were stationed at Fort Myer in Arlington, Virginia, right outside of Washington, DC. The move shifted everything. Where Killeen pressed in with silence and threats, the D.C. area pulsed with energy, alive with music, culture, and possibility.

They settled into Tencza Terrace, a high-rise just outside the gates of Fort Myer, filled with military families and young couples like themselves, balancing duty with the first chapters of parenthood.

Hallways carried the sound of children running between apartments, neighbors borrowing sugar or watching each other's kids, and weekend barbecues spilling out into the courtyards and concrete play lots.

The elevators were notoriously janky, sometimes opening between floors, sometimes revealing nothing but a brick wall. Nobody panicked or treated it like a malfunction. At Tencza Terrace, it was just another day.

Families felt safe there, a sharp contrast to today's

parenting practices. Parents thought nothing of letting their children trick-or-treat through the entire building while adults enjoyed a holiday party in the community room on the first floor.

Adrienne, just five years old, once went door to door in costume, clutching her little pumpkin candy bucket. In the stairwell, she came face to face with a stranger in a mask. Terrified, she dropped her bucket and bolted, screaming as tears streamed down her face.

The man gave chase, and Adrienne, running for dear life, did not stop until she burst into the adult party downstairs. Spotting her father, she leapt into his arms, burying her face in the safety of his chest.

When she dared to look up, the masked stranger stood there sheepishly, holding out the pumpkin bucket. Apologizing for frightening her, he explained that he had only been trying to return the candy she dropped in the stairwell.

The terror of that moment etched itself permanently into Adrienne's memory. The fear was real, the pounding of her heart as she tore down those stairs unforgettable. But pressed into her father's chest, she felt an unshakable sense of safety, as if nothing could touch her so long as his arms were around her.

Adrienne was Daddy's Little Girl. To her, Barry represented strength, stability, and pride. He was her first image of what it meant to feel protected. Many who knew them believed she favored her father, and they were right. He was her favorite parent, until he wasn't.

Life as a military child came naturally to her, but watching her father leave never got easier.

Each time orders came, Adrienne packed her little green suitcase, certain that if she was ready fast enough, he would take her along. But no matter how carefully she folded her clothes, she always ended up watching him walk away. Every departure ended the same, her tears at the gate, his promise to see them soon, her mother's gentle pull back toward the car.

She did not know that all those goodbyes were rehearsals. One day, his leaving would be permanent, and all the earlier departures had only been practice.

That longing for security, first felt at the gate and later in the stairwell when the masked man chased her, never truly left her. It shaped how she loved and how she feared. Safety, for Adrienne, would always look like her father's arms and sound like his voice telling her she was okay.

Inside their apartment, blacklight art glowed, and Zodiac Lovers posters hung side by side, Barry's Virgo steady and disciplined, Sandra's Aquarius radiant and untamed. The series was known for its erotic illustrations, each zodiac rendered in sexual positions, more bedroom fantasy than living room art.

For most households, they would have been too risqué to hang on the wall. For Barry and Sandra, they were a declaration. They were not a typical couple, and their love was anything but ordinary. He grounded her, she lifted him, and together they found a flow that made their passion and devotion impossible to miss.

On another wall hung the Jaws poster, a souvenir from taking five-year-old Adrienne to see the blockbuster that defined an era. It never crossed Barry and Sandra's minds that the film might be wildly inappropriate for a child, or that displaying the poster afterward would mean Adrienne lived with a daily reminder of what had terrified her. To them, it was simply a keepsake from a shared experience, after all they were still young adults.

For Adrienne, though, the shark's gaping jaws and lifeless eyes burrowed into her imagination.

The fear lingered, echoing the stairwell chase on Halloween night.

Those shocks imprinted more than fright; they etched the conviction that her father's arms were the only place she could truly breathe again. That sense of safety, fleeting and fragile, became the foundation of her bond with him, shaping how she reached for his protection even as the years made it harder to find.

Barry and Sandra's biggest worry as parents in Chocolate City was Adrienne's uncontrolled asthma. Sandra often rushed her down to the clinic on the post when the wheezing grew too tight to ignore.

For Adrienne, it became the burden of childhood, an illness triggered by almost anything: running too fast, laughing too hard, even the air around her. But more than likely, it was the cigarette smoke that lingered in the house. Barry was a smoker, and that only made things worse.

Their approaches to the illness revealed a deeper divide in how they saw the world. Sandra leaned toward homeopathic remedies, teaching Adrienne how to calm herself and control her breathing. Barry believed medicine was the answer, that the rescue inhaler should always be within reach.

The clash over how to treat Adrienne's asthma was one of their most persistent disagreements, a reminder that even in their shared love for their daughter, their visions often split.

Five years after Adrienne's birth, their second child arrived, a ten-pound baby boy. Barry Jr. was big from the start, his size foreshadowing the presence and personality he would carry through life.

He was born in April 1974, the same month Hank Aaron broke Babe Ruth's home-run record, shattering barriers in baseball. With his birth, Barry and Sandra carried on the family's tradition of names: Barry, George, and John, stretching back to 1929, a legacy that would one day continue through Barry Jr.'s own son. The five-year spacing between Adrienne and Barry Jr. was deliberate, giving them time to grow as parents and steady their marriage.

Life in the D.C. area offered something entirely different from Texas. Chocolate City was alive, its music, fashion, and energy spilling out of U Street and Georgia Avenue. Go-go bands like Chuck Brown and the Soul Searchers were defining a new sound, while Frankie Beverly and Maze were just beginning to break through, soon to become D.C.'s adopted favorites. They were not yet the anthem makers they would become, but their early shows hinted at the soul and energy that would one day fill RFK Stadium and echo through every Black family reunion.

Barry and Sandra went to D.C.'s U Street corridor, a central hub for African American culture and nightlife in the 1970s, alive with music, dance, and style. They caught the artists on their way up, before they were legends, when the music still felt like a secret passed among the young and hungry. For young African Americans, D.C. was a cultural capital, a city that belonged to them, pulsing with pride and possibility.

Neither of them were big drinkers; beer, wine, or liquor only appeared on rare occasions when they entertained. Adrienne never remembers seeing either of her parents drunk. Music was their indulgence, their release, the thing that followed them home from U Street and Georgia Avenue. It filled the house after nights out and lingered long after the needle lifted.

But it was not only the nightlife.

Day to day, Barry and Sandra built a family tempo within the capital's pulse. Adrienne started school, making friends in the playgrounds of the apartment complex.

Sandra never stopped loving fashion; she stitched clothes

late into the night while prepping Adrienne for photo shoots in the local military life magazine, brushing her hair, pressing her dresses, and teaching her how to smile for the camera.

She poured that love into her family, sewing matching outfits for portraits, her designs a quiet signature woven into their story. Barry balanced Army duty with weekend trips to the Wharf, hauling back crabs that became feasts around their table.

Sundays meant church, followed by drives through Rock Creek Park, windows rolled down, WOL radio carrying the sound of D.C. soul. Even in the modest spaces of their high-rise apartment, there was a sense of expansion, of being part of something larger than themselves.

Life in D.C. was fun and lively, rooted in music, routine, and love. When the next set of orders arrived, they packed up to move again, this time to a foreign land that would open them up to a new world and culture.

## CHAPTER 9
# K-TOWN

When the Army moved them again, their world stretched farther than they could have imagined.

Germany was next. Barry was stationed in Kaiserslautern, known as K-Town, and Sandra found herself raising children in a foreign country where she stood out everywhere she went.

She quickly adapted, turning Army quarters into a home, stretching dollars, cooking meals that smelled like home. She made sure the children always had their own space, creating playrooms even if only in a closet. The household ran like a system, purging items every season, keeping only what was needed, always ready to pack up the house in a weekend if Barry got the call.

K-Town was its own world, a mix of American structure and European pace. Military life filled every corner, from the rumble of post buses to the chatter of children enjoying their young, secure existence.

For Black families, it was a rare kind of peace, a break from the tension they had known back home. Race did not disappear, but it softened. Locals watched them with curiosity more than judgment, and soldiers often said Europe felt like breathing air that was not laced with animosity.

Weekends were filled with cookouts, record players spinning Earth, Wind & Fire and the Commodores, while kids ran between apartments flying kites. In Germany, kite flying was a simple joy, with wide open fields, steady winds, and bright colors dancing against the gray sky giving the children a sense of freedom that matched the music.

The commissary and the post exchange became gathering points, places to trade stories and recipes, to find small pieces of home on foreign shelves. Black women, often isolated from extended family, leaned on each other, creating sisterhoods that held them through long deployments and lonely nights. Sandra found her place among them, her easy laughter and sense of order drawing others in.

Germany became an experience none of them would forget.

Adrienne's school sat high on a hill, often wrapped in fog. Each morning, Sandra walked her to the bottom, and Adrienne made the climb alone. She often turned back, watching her mother disappear into the mist, her figure fading until she was gone.

That image imprinted itself deep, so deep that years later Adrienne would dream of it, replaying the fog swallowing her mother again and again.

It was in Germany that the world opened wider for Adrienne. When Alex Haley's Roots aired, the military school required every student to gather in the gymnasium and sit on the floor to watch.

Day after day, for a week, they followed Kunta Kinte, Fiddler, Kizzy, and Chicken George. For Adrienne, it was the first raw introduction to slavery and African American history, the first time the past felt personal.

She never forgot the moment when, after many years apart, Chicken George finally returned home to Kizzy. Kizzy's joy was so pure and overwhelming that she looked as if her heart might burst from the force of it.

To Adrienne, it was the most romantic thing she had ever seen. That kind of love, powerful enough to survive distance, pain, and time, stayed with her. She hoped that one day she would know a love like that, one that made her heart race the same way. And she did.

The movie might have been the spark that shaped her future. It awakened something deeper than curiosity, a connection to history that would guide her life's path. In time, she built a career dedicated to preserving memories and safeguarding stories, deepening her devotion to the power of history and the people who keep it alive.

Life abroad left its own set of memories, moments that Adrienne still carries with her.

During one tennis lesson, she and another girl ran for the same ball. Adrienne reached it first, but as the other girl turned away, she swung her racket back and hit Adrienne in the mouth. Adrienne wasn't sure if it was on purpose, but it felt like it. The blow broke her tooth. Barry was furious, calling it careless and refusing to let her return.

The lessons ended, but the moment stayed with her. She never forgot the taste of blood, the shock of pain, and her father's anger. Even years later, she obsessed over her teeth, brushing carefully, keeping every dental appointment, and hoping the veneer that was carefully crafted for her front tooth never comes loose and betrays her.

Sandra signed Adrienne up for Girl Scouts to help them connect with other military families. Through USA Girl Scouts

Overseas (USAGSO), she joined the Kaiserslautern Community 555 troop, a program designed for the children of military and American expatriate families living abroad. The organization provided a familiar sense of community, offering camps and activities that helped bridge the distance from home.

When the family returned to the United States, Sandra continued her involvement and became a troop leader. The girls called her Lucy.

Adrienne stayed in Girl Scouts through Brownies, Juniors, and Cadettes. By eighth grade, she and her friend Marcia begged their mothers not to make them continue into high school. After much convincing, both mothers agreed. Adrienne often joked that she felt like the oldest Girl Scout in the country by the time she hung up her sash.

Back in New Jersey, the troop camped every season at Camp Sacajawea in Farmingdale, less than ten minutes from the Garden State Parkway. The camp was owned and operated by the Girl Scouts of the Jersey Shore.

The highlight of every trip was winning the lottery for the lakeside cabin, warm and cozy in the winter, cool and breezy in the summer.

When luck didn't strike, the girls prepared to rough it in platform tents and sleeping bags, hoping the daddy long leg spiders stayed away and no one had to make a bathroom run in the freezing dark.

Summer hikes carried the constant risk of ticks, and everyone had to be checked carefully at the end of the day.

It was all part of the experience Sandra wanted her daughter to have, discipline, teamwork, and adventure, no matter where the military sent them.

In Germany, volksmarches became a family ritual, long walks through forests and villages that ended with medals for the children and friendships for Barry and Sandra. They built bonds with other military families that lasted decades, even across continents. The pattern of military life continued: structured, predictable, and comforting in its repetition.

Barry's love and appreciation for Sandra remained steady a decade into their marriage and even longer if you count their high school courtship. While stationed in Germany, he had a jacket made as a declaration of their love, black love. Though mainstream America often tried to dismiss or distort it, those who lived it knew it was real, precious, and enduring.

The jacket was black wool, customized with hand-stitched and appliqué designs. Across the upper back, in white block letters, it read "TO MY WIFE OF LOVE." Below it was an embroidered image of a raised Black Power fist rising from the continent of Africa, outlined in red, black, and green with a yellow lightning bolt behind it. Each sleeve carried the Pan-African flag in horizontal stripes, and the right sleeve featured a large brown appliqué fist. At the bottom, it read "KAISERSLAUTERN, GERMANY, 77-80," marking the years they spent stationed there.

The jacket was both a love letter and a statement of identity, blending Barry's devotion to Sandra with his pride in their culture and their shared journey abroad. It told the story of a young couple who believed their love could outlast anything, distance, duty, and time.

No one could have imagined how a love like this could break, how something so deeply rooted could slowly erode beneath the strain of unmet expectations, unspoken pain, and the quiet distance that sometimes grows between two people who once shared everything.

The jacket remained, a silent witness to a love once fierce and unshakable.

In June 1978, Barry and Sandra welcomed their third child. Carlos was born in Frankfurt, Germany, a surprise they kept to themselves until their return to the States. When they arrived, they carried with them not only stories of life overseas but also a new baby no one expected.

Sandra, who hadn't named her first child, decided she would create her own rhythm with the next two. She made sure their names moved in sync: Adrienne, Barry, and Carlos, the "ABC kids" she affectionately called them. That pattern gave her a quiet sense of authorship, a way to leave her own mark on the family's unfolding story.

The return to the States marked another shift. Military life meant constant motion, but this move carried more weight. They were no longer a young couple chasing new adventures. They were a family of five, seasoned by deployments, distance, and discovery, carrying Germany in their memories like a story they would never quite leave behind.

## CHAPTER 10
# CELEBRATE GOOD TIMES

Barry's next set of orders brought the family back to familiar ground in New Jersey.

His assignment to Fort Monmouth marked both a homecoming and a new chapter. The installation sat in Monmouth County, surrounded by the towns of Eatontown, Tinton Falls, and Oceanport, only a few miles from the Atlantic Ocean.

It would be his final post, the place where his military career came full circle.

Years later, the base would close and transform into the site of a major Netflix film production campus, but in those days, it was still alive with soldiers, families, and the rhythm of military life that had shaped their world.

Fort Monmouth was its own world. The base had a bowling alley, a movie theater, a commissary stocked with familiar comforts, and bike trails that seemed endless to young legs.

The children loved the freedom, roaming between playgrounds and the field house with the safety of armed guards always nearby. To them, the Army didn't mean deployments and drills; it meant Saturday matinees, birthday parties, and summer afternoons under the Jersey sun.

Freedom, though, came with its dangers. One hot afternoon, Adrienne and Barry Jr. roamed the base their friends, chasing the thrill of exploring places they weren't supposed to go. Their wandering led them to a wide drainage pipe jutting out over a shallow ditch, its dark mouth daring them to enter.

On their hands and knees, they crawled inside. The air was damp and cool against their arms as the daylight behind them shrank. Their laughter echoed off the walls until someone froze. The pipe wasn't empty. The walls were alive with slick, black leeches clinging to the concrete.

Screams filled the tunnel. Panic set in. The children shoved forward, knees slipping on wet concrete, hands scraping against the rough surface, desperate to reach the circle of light at the far end. Each drip of water made them imagine leeches dropping from above.

They spilled out of the pipe in a heap, soaked and shaking, slapping at their arms and legs to be sure nothing had stuck. Relief came when no one found a leech, but it quickly turned into another kind of fear.

If their parents knew, they'd be in trouble and none of them had a good answer for why they went in at all. Shaken and more afraid of their parents than the leeches, they swore to keep the whole thing quiet.

It was one of those moments that showed how childhood freedom carried both risk and reward, a memory folded into the good times right alongside the laughter and the music.

New Jersey also meant family.

For them, the Parkway was a living thread that tied together duty at Fort Monmouth and family roots up north.

In North Jersey, places like Newark, East Orange, and

Irvington held their roots. It was where grandparents, aunts, uncles, and cousins lived, where holidays brought everyone together, and where Sunday drives or summer trips meant piling into the car and heading up and down the Garden State Parkway.

Toll booths marked the pace of travel, coins ringing out as they dropped into steel baskets. Traffic moved like a tide, endless streams of cars carrying people toward the shore or back to the city. Radio stations faded in and out, voices and songs stitching together memories mile by mile. It carried them to reunions filled with food, laughter, and stories that stretched across generations.

To Barry, Fort Monmouth meant routine. His days followed a steady order, guided by duty and discipline yet eased by the comfort of family close by.

For Sandra, it was a season of settling. She could finally create her own systems, free from the uncertainty of another move.

At 8 Gosslin Avenue, their life found a pattern that felt almost permanent.

Sundays anchored that routine. Black-eyed peas simmered low on the stove, Uncle Ben's white rice, Jiffy cornbread cut into neat squares. Red Kool-Aid filled the pitcher, cold and unmistakable, the color alone enough to signal the day.

Sandra's dedication to that meal mirrored her dedication to the relationship itself. Showing up, consistently, mattered to her. At the table, Barry was strict about manners. No elbows. No singing. Clean your plate before you drank your juice.

Sandra loved her time in Germany and filled their home with reminders of it. The alabaster lamps glowed softly in the evenings. The German clock ticked steadily on the wall. The towering schrank, a large wooden wardrobe for clothes and linens, anchored the living room.

Behind its glass doors, her German glassware sparkled like jewels, though she never poured a drink from them. The silver remained polished and perfect, more for display than for use, a reflection of her care and pride.

Even the drawer of Volksmarch medals, neatly stacked and tucked away, told its own story, symbols of places walked, lessons learned, and a family that carried every stop of the journey home with them.

Years later, if you asked, Sandra could still speak some German she learned overseas.

The schools reflected what had always mattered: Swimming River Elementary, Tinton Falls Middle, Monmouth Regional High. Each classroom was filled with the children of soldiers, sailors, and airmen. Military life taught kids to adapt, to be resilient, and to find connection wherever they landed.

School was already a family focus; homework, tests, and classroom stories were regular topics at home. Report cards were celebrated with cash incentives from Sandra: five dollars for every A, three for every B, one for every C. When teachers sent notes home, Barry did not simply sign them. He wrote back, offering his opinion on the assignment or the grade.

Barry's Army story closed in 1980, a decision he made after sixteen years of steady service.

Promotions stalled, and rather than continue to wait, he chose to retire on his own terms. He had given the Army his youth, his discipline, and his loyalty; now it was time to invest those things in his family.

When Barry retired, Kool & The Gang had just released *Celebration*. The song floated through the neighborhood, all joy and feel-good energy, the kind of soundtrack that made people laugh, gather, and believe good times could stretch far into the future.

For a moment, the song fit. It marked the end of constant moves, deployments, and separations. It sounded like freedom.

But the celebration was short-lived.

Barry realized quickly that work outside of the military was different.

He would come to realize that the Army had been his lifeline, the structure that kept him steady. Outside its order, the ground felt uncertain. Stripped of the system that defined him, Barry felt the weight of that loss.

One of his first jobs after leaving the military was a paper route for the *Star-Ledger*. It may seem unusual for an adult to have a paper route, but by the 1980s the traditional model was already shifting. While children still delivered papers in many towns, newspapers increasingly hired adults for early morning routes, believing they were more dependable for predawn deliveries. It was a transition period, the beginning of the end for the classic after-school paper route, though it had not disappeared yet.

Although the *Star-Ledger* is based in Newark, it had the largest circulation in the state of New Jersey and was delivered throughout Monmouth County. Barry often took the kids with him on his morning paper runs, tossing papers onto porches, watching for dogs, and hoping to collect the cash envelopes on Sundays to get paid.

He served as the Circulation Manager for the area. Adrienne's classmate Michael worked as one of the carriers. In many Monmouth County towns, the paperboy system was still very much alive, with children delivering newspapers by bicycle after school or in the early morning hours, even as adults increasingly filled the earliest routes.

Michael was one of Adrienne's fondest friends even at eleven years old, and that remained so throughout high school and after. He was the first of two white guys she ever felt close to; it wasn't a romantic closeness, it was an "I see you" closeness.

He was kind, funny, and seemed to genuinely like her, not because she was Black, not because she was a girl, but just because she was Adrienne. She liked him too; even as a little kid, she always loved his smile, he was just fun.

Truth be told, Adrienne hasn't known a Michael she didn't like Michael Jackson, Michael Jordan, Michael Bivens, Michael that lived across the street, Uncle Michael, Cousin Michael, the baseball player Michael she dated in college, Michael B. Jordan the actor.

And then one day, she felt it. Her heart raced so quickly it almost burst. She found her Michael.

He was from California.

An East Coast life, a West Coast heart, two coasts meeting like rival verses, never meant to harmonize, yet somehow landing on the same beat.

The detail lingered with her. California had been written into her story long before she understood what it meant. Now it stood in front of her, human and undeniable.

The feeling itself was familiar, echoing something she first learned years earlier in Germany, watching *Roots*, when she understood that real love could survive distance, pain, and time.

Their relationship was complicated, intense, and deeply emotional.

She jokingly compared them to the Julia Michaels song *Issues*, not for the words themselves but for the spirit of it.

They loved hard, fought hard, and somehow always circled back to each other. Their connection was raw and imperfect, full of passion, stubbornness, forgiveness, and the kind of honesty that could both heal and hurt.

She married him.

Friends and family had tickets on the Adrienne and Michael roller coaster because they were all along for the ride.

At their wedding reception, instead of a toast, it turned into a roast filled with jokes and warnings that they would both be disowned if divorce ever crossed their minds.

After more than twenty years, he remains her soul tie, a bond that exists beyond logic or distance. It is a connection that runs deep, where emotion, memory, and spirit intertwine so tightly that neither of them can ever fully let go.

## CHAPTER II
# THE FRUIT BOWL

Before reality TV arrived, the Jersey Shore belonged to families, neighbors, church picnics, corner stores, schools, boardwalks, and backyards. They lived it. They claimed it.

Then MTV turned it into a caricature of fist pumps, tanning oil, and sloppy nights out. That show never told the real story, the story of the families who lived, worked, studied, and built lives along the 141 miles of coastline from Perth Amboy to Cape May.

The so-called reality was scripted chaos packaged as truth, and too many mistook it for real life. It captured the loudest, sloppiest moments and branded an entire place with that image.

The truth that shaped generations was quieter and more complicated. It was parents working double shifts, grandparents keeping traditions alive, kids running through backyards, and neighbors watching out for each other. That was the story worth telling, the one that never made it on TV but left a lasting mark.

So, when people from the area are asked where they're from, they don't soften it. They answer plain, "We're from the Jersey Shore. Don't judge us."

Because the Shore was never a punchline. It was community. It was pride.

When Barry retired, the family moved a few miles down the road to Tinton Falls.

Their section was predominantly Black, a tight-knit corner just 0.17 square miles on the edge of town, across the street from Red Bank.

Within that section sat the Fruit Bowl. Streets named Apple, Peach, Cherry, Plum, and Pear.

The family didn't live on a fruit street, but they were part of it all the same. The Fruit Bowl wasn't only geography; it was identity. At its center was the Field, the heartbeat of the neighborhood.

Kids cut through backyards to get there, sneakers streaked with grass stains, because the Field was where everything happened. Basketball games, first crushes, gossip sessions, boom boxes blasting until the streetlights demanded curfew. It didn't matter what you had or didn't have. The Field belonged to the Fruit Bowl, and in turn, it belonged to something bigger.

When the days stretched long and the air turned heavy with summer heat, the Field came alive. That was when the neighborhood pulsed with energy, when laughter drowned out the sound of cicadas and every evening felt like a block party waiting to happen.

Summers never felt endless. Kids knew the clock was ticking, so they squeezed in every ounce of fun before it was gone. Cousins came down from North Jersey or out of state, Angel, Cheryl, Donna, George, Jamillah, Kevin, Kim, Michael, Muncie, Nadine, Rahim, Rashaan, Sabrina, Saffiyah, Sandy, Shamond, Sherri, Sherrica, Taheerah and Tracey.

Everyone felt loose, alive, and free. The air carried its own rhythm: school out, streets buzzing, laughter spilling into the night.

Meetups at the Eatontown Roller Rink were a regular part of the vibe, where skating was optional, but socializing was mandatory. Days were spent at Great Adventure in Jackson, chasing roller coasters, funnel cakes, and concerts that stretched long into the night.

Weekends belonged to the Asbury Park and Long Branch boardwalks, where the salt air and neon lights painted their childhood in joy. Trips to Englishtown were for school clothes shopping, a family ritual that marked the end of summer and the start of another school year.

They were loud. They were visible. They were free.

Looking back, it was clear: pure summer madness.

Adrienne's first summer concert was New Edition. She and her friends loved *Candy Girl, Mr. Telephone Man,* and *Popcorn Love.*

Ronnie, Bobby, Ricky, and Mike each wore a different colored vest with a matching headband. She was close enough to the front to feel like part of the show. When they threw the headbands into the crowd, Adrienne caught Ricky's green one. Later, she cut the headband into pieces and added snaps to make wristbands for her friends.

One day, a neighborhood girl came over with her cousin visiting from down south. They hung out in Adrienne's room, where the walls were covered from corner to corner with posters from *Word Up* and *Right On* magazines. Adrienne proudly showed them her wristband. When she wasn't looking, the cousin slipped it into her pocket and took it home.

When Adrienne confronted the neighbor, she admitted the cousin had stolen it. Since the cousin was already back down south, Adrienne knew she would never get it back. It became a lesson about trust, a reminder that not everyone deserved access to the things that mattered most.

Even racism barely touched them then. They knew it existed, this was still America, but in school most were military kids, protected by that shared bond. Instead of the active shooter drills of today, the only drills were fire drills.

They lived in a bubble of joy, camaraderie, and innocence.

The Shore gave them a sense of belonging. The Fruit Bowl gave them identity. The Field gave them freedom.

But the Avenue gave them a home.

The Avenue was more than a street; it was a declaration. Their street, their foundation, their families. The Artises, Austins, Catleys, Goodes, Harrises, Joneses, Perrys, Pullings, Smiths, Summys and Woodses

Together, they were a crew. The Avenue Family for life.

Depending on what song topped the charts that week, Michael the neighbor could be heard on the curb with his boom box, blasting music into the open air while the kids danced and played until the streetlights flickered on. He was always quick to drop a rap verse, eager to prove his skills.

Some families on the street were Jehovah's Witnesses, which meant they weren't supposed to mix too closely with the "worldly" kids.

But rules bent on the Avenue.

Jimmy ignored the rules completely. He was out there almost every evening, cracking jokes, laughing hard, moving through the block as if none of those restrictions applied to him.

And then there were kids like Julian, who didn't even live in the Fruit Bowl but always drifted over to the Avenue. He knew that's where the pulse was, where the music, the laughter, and the energy spilled out onto the pavement.

He wasn't the only one hanging out on the Avenue. Aisha,

Beep, Charlene, Donald, Eric, June, Kym, LaQuita, Marcia, Necee, Price, Rodney, Todd, Tonya, Wendy, and Yha'ru all found themselves there too, adding to the mix and making the block feel even fuller.

Jokes came easy in that crowd, and laughter carried down the street.

They cracked up at just about everything and everyone, like Paul, who was forever running late for the bus or his ride to school, tripping over himself because he was still lacing up the sneakers he had scrubbed clean the night before.

No one was spared, so you'd better be ready with your comeback if you set foot on the Avenue.

None of the parents ever told them to clear the streets. Without sidewalks, there was nowhere else for them to go, and few adults wanted their neatly trimmed lawns trampled by a pack of kids.

They never realized the missing sidewalks were a marker of suburban privilege. Sidewalks, after all, belonged to city neighborhoods where people walked, took buses, and lived closer to the ground.

Suburban planners imagined cars would define these streets, keeping foot traffic and the riffraff out. What no one anticipated was that the children of the Avenue would claim the blacktop as their own, turning it into a playground, a dance floor, and a stage.

It was on that stretch of pavement, between front porches and parked cars, that friendships were born and childhoods took shape.

Like so many bonds formed on that block, Adrienne's friendship with Kimmy became one of the defining stories of her youth. Though Kimmy was two years older, she never treated Adrienne like the younger tagalong. From her bedroom window, Adrienne could look straight across to Kimmy's room next door.

The two spent hours leaning out across the narrow gap, trading stories, laughing at the latest school drama, and dissecting episodes of Little House on the Prairie. Their chatter floated into the night air, weaving itself into the soundtrack of the Avenue, another strand in the web of family and memory that defined the block.

Adrienne admired Kimmy deeply. She was good at everything: sports, school, and people. Everyone liked her.

Kimmy was a natural athlete who played sports year-round and could rival any boy in the neighborhood.

Basketball and track were her favorites. She modeled excellence in women's sports long before it became popular, along with Audrey, Delinda, Dollie, Lajuana, Linda, Roslyn, Stacey and Teresa.

Kimmy is the reason Adrienne loves track and field today. Kimmy always pushed Adrienne to do more. One year she bet Adrienne that she couldn't make the track team and stay on it for the entire season.

Adrienne accepted the challenge even though she was the slowest runner on the team, she did it.

With asthma and limited lung capacity, she struggled through every practice. Long distance, short distance, long jump, she wasn't good at any of it. Her nerves didn't help either; she was often disqualified from meets for false starts, unable to anticipate the sound of the gun.

But she stayed on the team and won the bet. It was the first time Adrienne reached beyond her grasp, and although she didn't excel, crossing the finish line meant something. It proved she could endure.

Kimmy was funny and fearless, and if anyone ever messed with Adrienne, she was the first to come to her defense. Adrienne felt like they were soul sisters because their mothers shared a birthday.

February 7th became one of Adrienne's favorite days because she could celebrate four of her favorite people, her mother, Sandra, Kimmy's mom, Julian, and Tonya.

Years later, when Adrienne's husband met Kimmy, he called her "Kim Possible," like the Disney Channel hero, because there was nothing she couldn't do. The name fit perfectly.

That bond was unspoken and unshakable.

As the kids grew older, the energy shifted from the streets to the basements of the parents cool enough to tolerate them.

The Avenue was known for its basement parties. The basements felt like speakeasies, hidden spaces that came alive after dark, where music, laughter, and freedom flowed away from watchful eyes.

Jermel and Matt opened their doors, Andie, who they all called "Cap" hosted parties at the end of the street, and the Woods' basement was part of the lineup too. Matt and Sonny took turns on the turntables, carrying the crowd from one basement to the next, while Cap always seemed to find a variety of DJs to keep his parties fresh.

The gatherings grew so popular that at any given time there could be three different parties rocking the Avenue in a single month, especially in the summertime. It was party after party after party, a season of music, sweat, and joy.

Those were the good old days, when the Avenue wasn't just a street, but the lifeblood of their youth.

As they reveled in their carefree days, choices were being made that carried consequences that would eventually destroy their idyllic existence. They had no idea that every laugh, every dance, and every sun-soaked afternoon would one day shatter.

## CHAPTER 12
# WHEN BARRY MET HALLE

Co-worker relationships were a trap as old as the workplace itself.
History is full of stories about lines crossed on the job, and when Barry met Halle, it was no different.

He had always flirted, always strayed. He liked to joke that he belonged to the "Four F Club": find them, feel them, fuck them, and forget them.

Less than a year after leaving the military, his poor decision making became clear.

Halle wasn't the first woman he betrayed Sandra with, but she would be the last.

He was her boss, older, married, and Black. She was young, white, and defiant.

At thirty-five, Barry supervised thirteen Cumberland Farms stores across New Jersey. Halle, twenty-one, managed the Toms River location he had hired her to run. On paper, it was routine, but it was a setup for disaster, a bomb waiting to detonate.

The hazards stacked high. He had a wife and children at

home. She was barely out of her teens, still living with her mother, reckless and unbothered.

By the mid-1980s, corporations were already writing policies on "fraternization," rules meant to stop supervisors from crossing lines with staff. Courts were beginning to call it harassment, and even a rumor could wreck a career.

Then there was the greater risk: race. A Black man and a white woman together even in 1980s New Jersey carried a heavy cost. Every glance, every whisper, every question held danger. A look from a stranger, a murmur from a clerk, the wrong move could change everything. Barry knew it, and so did Halle. Neither cared.

For Halle, rebellion was oxygen. Dating Black men was her protest, her way of saying no to the rules that bound her house. Barry let himself get pulled in. Because she had dated Black men before, he convinced himself it wasn't taboo. The truth was simpler. He was fascinated. No White woman had ever given him the time of day, let alone a young blonde one.

She knew he was married. She knew there were children at home. To her, that was his burden, not hers.

There were no dinners, no movies, no romance. Just sex. Most of it happened in the storage room in the back of the store, shelves stacked with boxes, the buzz of freezers behind them, Barry slipping away under the pretense of work. He was a supervisor reducing himself to hurried encounters behind a stockroom door, covering lust with invoices and schedules.

Then Halle quit. No warning, no explanation. One day she was the manager, the next she was gone. Her leaving stripped away their cover but didn't end the affair.

Now every meeting was deliberate, every move riskier. They started using her mother's house. Halle knew when her mother would be gone and when she'd return. Barry would slip in, get what he came for, and sneak out before the front door opened. That should have humiliated him most, a married man with children creeping out of his twenty-one-year-old girlfriend's mother's house like a teenager.

But shame never stopped him. Lust smothered it. The danger only pulled him deeper. Without the cover of work, it turned into pure obsession. Each visit chipped away another piece of his life.

Barry told himself he was in control, chasing the thrill, choosing the risk. The truth was Halle set the terms. She dictated when and where. She opened doors and closed them. Barry followed her, mistaking his weakness for power.

Halle liked it that way. She baited him, lured him, watched him crawl back for more. To her it was sport, testing how far she could make a grown, married man risk his family, his job, even his freedom.

One night showed how fragile his illusion was. They were in a park, clothes half-off, lost in the rush. Blue and red lights flashed, a knock at the window, a flashlight slicing through the dark. A Black man, half-naked, caught with a White woman; that story could end in handcuffs, a mugshot, maybe worse.

But the officer didn't look at Barry. He looked at Halle. "Are you okay? Is everything alright?" In that moment, Barry's marriage, his children, his job, even his freedom balanced on one word from her.

She said "yes." The cop backed away, and the danger dissolved into the night.

Barry sat there, pants still undone, realizing how close he had come to losing it all. The cruel truth was plain: he was never in control. Halle held the power from the start.

And still, he didn't stop. Even after staring into the glare of the cop's flashlight, he kept chasing her, willing to risk everything for one more taste of the thrill.

## CHAPTER 13
# THE CHICKENS CAME HOME

What do you expect when you have unprotected sex? After six months of sneaking around, the inevitable happened. The chickens came home to roost; their actions finally brought the consequences they had set in motion.

Barry never forgot the moment. They were sitting in a bar, smoke curling, glasses sweating on the table. Halle had one of her sisters beside her, like a bodyguard. She didn't ease into it or ask him what he thought.

She just said it flat: I'm pregnant.

His mind flooded. He had a wife, children, and a whole life already in motion. And now Halle was placing a live grenade in his lap and pulling the pin. He could hardly remember what words he managed in reply, but the thoughts were loud: I'm trapped. This can't be real.

It felt like a car racing down a cliff with no brakes.

Barry knew the truth. Unprotected sex led here. He gambled anyway and lost. Still, in his twisted logic, it was the woman's job to not get pregnant. He was furious at Halle for letting it happen and even angrier at himself for being careless enough to risk it.

Her sister leaned in, sharp eyes, and asked the question he didn't want to face: "So what are your intentions?"

Barry stumbled, but it didn't matter. The choice wasn't his. Halle was calm, certain, defiant. She was keeping the baby.

Then her sister delivered the threat that sealed it: if Barry thought he could walk away, somebody was going to hurt him. Not a suggestion. Not a bluff. A promise.

Just like with the cop in the park, Barry's life tilted on Halle's word. Again, his fate wasn't his own.

But Halle hadn't factored in her mother. She hid the pregnancy as long as she could, clinging to the fantasy that Barry would rescue her.

She fooled herself into thinking their lust was love, that the baby would bind him to her forever. By then, Barry already had thirteen years of marriage and four children in his home. He was never going to leave.

And when her mother found out, the illusion collapsed. Halle's mother was a card-carrying racist, through and through. When she learned her daughter's baby was fathered by a Black man, she made her stance permanent: "You're not bringing that nigger baby into my house." That was the end of it.

Halle's only option was one of New Jersey's maternity homes, the kind where unwed mothers were hidden until delivery and then sent back into the world without their shame. Most were run by churches or social services. Outsiders saw charity. The girls inside felt exiled.

Life in those homes was rigid. Curfews. Chores. Silence about the fathers. They were told to repent, to be grateful, to carry their punishment quietly. Staff called it guidance. The girls called it survival.

Days crawled. Nights were long.

Every woman carried the same weight, waiting for labor, wondering what came next. Some planned to give their babies away. Others, like Halle, swore they would keep them.

At first, she believed keeping the baby would keep Barry. But with each month, the truth dug deeper. Barry wasn't coming. He wasn't leaving his wife. Every absence, every excuse made it clear. He wasn't hers, and neither was the future she imagined.

What had begun as hope ended in surrender.

She couldn't keep the baby in the maternity home forever. She couldn't go back to her mother's house with a Black child; her mother had already barred that door.

So, she made her decision: once the baby was born, she would place it in foster care. The only path was to walk out empty handed.

When Barry heard those words, it struck him harder than any flashlight or threat had before. The thought of his child, his blood, nameless in the system, passed from stranger to stranger, gutted him. Like the man-child he was, he turned to the one person who had always saved him: his mother.

Barry told his mother everything. As her only son, with four sisters around him, he was her center. She spoiled him, protected him, defended him. To him, she was more than a parent; she was his confidante. He had always trusted her to shield him.

So, when he told her about Halle, he expected the same. He confessed the affair, the pregnancy, his fear.

Dorothy didn't scold him, didn't tell him to stop, didn't push him to face reality. In her mind, Halle was temporary, a young white girl who would eventually go away. She believed it would pass and she wouldn't hang around.

When Barry expressed his despair about the baby going

into foster care, Dorothy acted. She decided the child would not end up in the system. She'd take the baby under her care.

Barry surrendered, as always. He fell into the comfort of being her child again, strapped in while she drove.

Eyes fixed ahead, hands steady on the wheel, Dorothy took control. Barry sat back, telling himself he was safe in her hands.

What he didn't see or refused to see was that she wasn't steering away from disaster. She was pressing harder on the gas, driving them all straight into it.

Dorothy moved quickly. She called it helping. In truth, it was control.

It was decided. His baby sister Janice, just eighteen years old, would take the baby and raise it as her own.

To the outside world, the child would be another grandchild, Janice's child. That lie would be the cement that held everything together.

## CHAPTER 14
# ASK NO QUESTIONS, TELL NO LIES

Barry moved through life certain that as Dorothy's only son, every sin he committed would be erased by her.

What he knew for sure was that his mother would handle it. She had always been the keeper of his sins, the one person who could take the weight of his recklessness and fold it neatly out of sight.

With her in charge, he could return to his wife and children, steady his voice, and carry on as though nothing had happened. The secret would not follow him home; it would be locked away in the vault of his mother's bosom, guarded with the same fierce loyalty that had shielded him all his life.

It was cowardice dressed up as problem-solving.

He didn't have the courage to tell Halle he wouldn't rescue her, he didn't have the courage to tell Sandra what he'd done, and he didn't have the courage to acknowledge the child as his own. Instead, he ducked every hard conversation and let Dorothy drive the lie.

The plan wasn't discussed; it was imposed. She wasn't

much different from Halle's mother. No, she wasn't a racist, but she was just as controlling.

Both women ruled through power and dependency.

Dorothy did not just create the plan, she drove it, like she was barreling down the Parkway.

She executed it with precision and at full speed, weaving through lanes, blowing past exits that might have led to another outcome.

She ran the tolls without a thought, racking up tickets that could have turned into warrants, not caring that debts or dangers might pile up as long as she kept moving forward.

She acted as if the rules did not apply to her at all, as if the road itself bent to her will.

Rest stops like Vince Lombardi, Alexander Hamilton, and Clara Barton flashed by like lifelines ignored. The long stretch of toll booths and exits became her highway of denial, each mile marker another secret pushed aside.

Barry sat in the passenger seat in silence, convincing himself the ride was safe, as if he alone had a seatbelt strapped tight while everyone else rode bare.

Janice did not fall into Dorothy's scheme by chance. An innocent visit to El Paso became another open road for Dorothy. She seized the moment, pulled Janice into the car, and pressed the gas.

In Barry's mind, this was the perfect solution. He convinced himself that Janice wanted a baby anyway, so giving her his child was a gift. He told himself it kept his family intact, kept his wife from finding out, and kept the child out of the system.

On paper, everyone won: Janice got the baby she supposedly longed for, he got to keep his marriage, and Dorothy kept the secret sealed.

Meanwhile, over 2,100 miles away, the opportunity Dorothy seized began with Franny.

Franny had eight children in East Orange, New Jersey. The older three refused to move out, making it harder to raise the younger five. Fed up, she told them if they wouldn't leave, she would, and she did. With help from her sister Laney and Laney's husband, Phillip; Franny packed up the younger children and moved to El Paso, Texas, leaving the older ones to fend for themselves.

At first, the move looked like a fresh start. But El Paso quickly became another struggle.

Franny clashed with Laney, her health began to fail with kidney disease, and raising her children in a new place weighed heavily. It was in the middle of this tension that Janice arrived to visit.

She found Franny homesick, eager to see their mother Dorothy in New Jersey. Back then airline tickets were transferable, so Janice handed Franny hers so she could make the trip home, expecting she'd return to her children and her life in Texas.

While Franny was gone, Laney made her move. With Franny weakened by illness and out of the way, she stripped the house without warning, relocating everyone to a friend's home as a temporary stop.

Once she and Phillip secured their own place, their treatment of Janice and the children turned nasty.

With no stable place to be, Janice circled back to the friend's house, waiting for Dorothy to send her a ticket to return home, unaware of the impending situation at home.

It wasn't Laney's maneuver that would decide Janice's future. That power still belonged to their mother.

Janice, suspended in uncertainty, was further disoriented

when Dorothy finally called. Her words carried no warmth, only calculation.

Barry had a baby with a white girl. The child was with the mother in a home for unwed mothers. When the girl leaves the maternity home, she plans to put the child in foster care.

Barry wanted to save his marriage. The solution was simple: Janice would return home so they could pick up the child before the girl was required to leave.

Dorothy spoke as if the decision was already made, leaving no room for refusal.

Janice listened and quietly accepted. Too immature to push back, too trusting of her mother to question, she took the order as fact. To her, it wasn't a negotiation; it was what her mother said would happen, and that was enough.

In truth, Janice didn't understand what had just been set in motion. She never thought about it as a life altering command but rather simple instructions from her mother.

Dorothy took her silence as compliance. No pushback, no hesitation, no risk of the plan unraveling. To her, Janice's quiet acceptance was proof enough that the matter was settled. The move was made, the piece was in place, and the cover was secured. And Janice, obedient as ever, prepared to do exactly what she was told.

Far from New Jersey, unseen, Janice was an easy cover. Dorothy saw more than a stranded daughter; she saw an opportunity. Janice's absence created a blank space. No one in New Jersey had seen her for months. That gap could be filled with a story: pregnancy, childbirth, and a baby. It didn't matter if it was true. What mattered was that people would believe it.

Dorothy picked Janice up from the airport, and they went straight to the maternity home. It was the first time either of them had laid eyes on Halle. She stepped outside carrying the baby, an eight-week-old girl. There was no greeting, no small talk, no pause. Halle placed the child in Janice's arms and said only, "Her name is Crystal Lee. Please don't change her name." Then she turned and walked away.

Janice never saw where she went. One moment Halle was there, the next she was gone, vanishing into the air like a ghost.

Janice held the baby close accepting the role her mother assigned her.

She walked away with Crystal pressed to her chest, the handoff complete, the silence absolute.

## CHAPTER 15
# WHEN YOU LEAST EXPECT IT

J anice had been watching the family's children since she was eleven. Babysitting came naturally to her, or at least that's what people thought.

By eighteen, no one questioned leaving a baby in her care.

For reasons hard to explain, people trusted her even though she was often mean and nasty. Adrienne saw it. So did her cousins.

Maybe it was because she grew up under Laney's bullying shadow.

The truth was simple. She was too young and too mean-spirited to be trusted with anyone's child.

Yet the family kept handing her the job. That said as much about their dysfunction as it did about her.

Her tongue was sharp. Her words were cruel.

She showed no compassion, not even for her own sister Franny. As Franny battled kidney disease, weak and fading, Janice didn't soften.

After a petty argument over a 7-Up soda and Janice's

refusal to call a medical van, she looked her sister in the eye and said, "I hope you die and turn in your grave." It wasn't anger. It was intent, a deliberate wound that cut deeper than the illness itself.

Sonny, Franny's fourth child, heard the argument and carried the weight of Janice's curse, never forgetting that his aunt had once wished his mother dead.

The sting of those words lingered long after the funeral.

Sonny also felt Dorothy's uncaring coldness. After Franny's death, she never addressed the children's grief or offered them comfort. Instead, she quickly divided them among relatives, leaving them to face their loss alone.

Before his mother passed, Sonny often visited Sandra and Barry on the Jersey Shore, spending a lot of time in their home. So, when Franny passed, taking him in felt natural to Sandra.

She drew him close and told him he would be coming home with them. Her compassion gave him a glimpse of stability he had never known. Still grieving, Sonny carried a fragile hope that in Sandra's home, with her warmth and Barry's steadiness, he might finally experience the love of a two-parent household. Although his grief lingered, he felt relief at the thought of safety, something he had never imagined for himself.

But in this family, safety never lasted.

Sandra never trusted Dorothy. Years of watching her manipulate situations, coddle her son, and show only selective warmth had taught her caution. Dorothy's care often came with conditions, and Sandra knew her children could easily become targets of her uncaring ways.

She only allowed visits to Dorothy's apartment reluctantly. There were plenty of cousins and laughter, but she hated the roach-infested building. She refused to risk bringing any of those critters home.

When it was time to leave, she stood outside shaking out every piece of clothing and their suitcase before anyone got in the car.

Deep down, she didn't believe Dorothy had her children's best interests at heart. It wasn't hatred. It was protection, Sandra's instinct to shield her children from a woman who could wound without raising her hand.

What Sandra didn't realize was that Janice was the one she should have been watching.

What she didn't know was that Janice had already planted fear in Adrienne many years earlier.

Their Tencza Terrace apartment held Adrienne's first memories of Janice as a babysitter. Janice couldn't have been older than twelve or thirteen, but to five-year-old Adrienne she seemed like an adult.

Adrienne begged her parents not to leave her with Janice, who forced her to stay in her room and remain silent the entire time they were gone.

One summer, a teenage male cousin came to visit. Adrienne was sitting on the floor playing with her toys when he came into the room and locked the door. He chased her, pushed her down, and laid on top of her. She screamed for Janice, knowing she could hear, but no help came. His weight crushed her voice until she could barely cry out. He was so heavy on her young body. Just before he could cross a line that could never be undone, Janice banged on the door and yelled for him to open it and to leave that child alone.

It wasn't the last time. It happened more than once before he was finally sent away.

Adrienne buried the memory deep, almost convincing herself it hadn't happened, until years later when she saw him again at a family cookout. The air left her lungs. Her chest tightened under the weight of what she remembered.

The fear returned, raw and familiar. She could still feel his heaviness.

She hated him for what he did, but she hated Janice more for letting it happen. That day etched another layer onto Adrienne's lifelong need for safety. Locks, routines, and control became her armor.

To this day, whenever Adrienne is home alone, she locks her bedroom door at night, even when the security system is armed. The habit is not about safety alone but about control, her way of keeping fear at bay.

She is easily startled, her nervous system stays on high alert, a state born from stress, anxiety, and trauma. Her body still remembers what her mind tries to forget, the fight-or-flight response always ready, guarding her from the possibility of someone coming into her room or surprising her when she least expects it.

So, her motto is "When you least expect it, expect it!"

The years passed, but the cruelty continued. With every visit, Janice found new ways to torment her.

Adrienne hadn't always been afraid of roaches; Janice made her that way.

She would stomp them out with Adrienne's own shoes, using each kill as an opportunity to be mean and to instill fear.

It wasn't about the bugs; it was about control. Janice seemed to enjoy watching Adrienne shrink, feeding on her discomfort. She had a cruel streak that showed early, a mix of envy, insecurity, and dominance wrapped in the innocence of youth. She liked having power over someone smaller, someone who couldn't fight back.

Janice's cruelty wasn't impulsive. It was deliberate.

She picked her moments, small acts that left lasting marks. A taunt, a glare, a slow smirk when she knew she had gotten inside your head. It was the kind of meanness that came from needing to feel superior, from wanting to hurt before being hurt.

Maybe her hatred wasn't about Adrienne at all. Maybe it was about Barry. The same resentment she held for her brother she found it easier to target his child. One thing was certain: Janice was always in the middle of the mess, starting it, stirring it, never far from the fallout.

Her mean streak ran deep.

Janice stirred trouble with phone calls, baiting relatives into gossip while Laney listened on the other line. At the right moment, Laney would jump in; louder, meaner, crueler turning whispers into full-blown war.

Together they cursed, manipulated, and pushed until they got their way. Laney wasn't balance; she was gasoline on Janice's fire.

Dorothy, Laney, and Janice moved as a pack, each one feeding the other's nastiness. There was nothing complicated about it.

Together they were deceptive, manipulative, and cruel.

## CHAPTER 16
# FEAR OF THE TRUTH

Janice was terrified of Sandra learning the truth.

Sandra welcomed her into her home, treated her like a little sister, never showing suspicion. That kindness made Janice's fear sharper. If Sandra ever discovered the truth, it would mean betrayal, not just exposure.

Whenever Janice brought Crystal to the Jersey Shore for cookouts or family gatherings, her nerves spiked.

Barry hovered too close, his eyes lingering on the child. Sandra noticed and snapped, "Why are you always up in that baby's face? You've got plenty of nieces and nephews you never pay attention to, why this one?"

Barry had no real answer. He looked away, brushing it off, but Sandra's sharp gaze caught what others ignored.

Janice was light-skinned, but the baby looked mixed race, different. The first cracks in the secret appeared at those gatherings, moments when Sandra's suspicions threatened to expose everything.

Dorothy's favoritism was loud, fierce, and unapologetic.

Sandra saw it clearly. She respected Dorothy as Barry's mother, but she knew their relationship was detrimental.

Sandra came from a different stock, a family that believed compassion was strength, not weakness.

Dorothy felt it every time she looked at her daughter-in-law; the difference, the breeding, the balance Sandra carried.

Dorothy resented her.

She resented Sandra's kindness most. She resented that Sandra embraced Dina, showing her love Dorothy herself had never given. She resented that Sandra welcomed Sonny, hugging him close after Franny died, offering him the stability Dorothy could not provide. Each act exposed the gap between them.

Sandra didn't need to say she was better; Dorothy already felt it.

That resentment further explained Dorothy's willingness to lie. She claimed she was helping Barry save his marriage, but she didn't care about his marriage, or about Sandra, or about the children.

She enjoyed the secrecy, the deception, the hurt it created. In her silence and schemes, she found satisfaction.

Dorothy's favoritism didn't just strain her relationship with Sandra; it also bred resentment between Barry and his younger sisters, especially Janice and Laney. Their bitterness had been building for years. Barry was Dorothy's chosen one, the golden boy who never faced consequences.

If anyone challenged him, Dorothy stood in front of him like a wall of iron, defending him even in fights she knew he had started. To Janice and Laney, Barry wasn't just their brother; he was their mother's prize, constant proof that they would never matter as much as her son.

Dorothy made the decision that Janice would take the baby, and everyone else was expected to fall in line.

Laney was furious. "Fuck him," she snapped. "Let him deal with it. He wanted to run around, and now everybody's stuck cleaning up his mess." Her anger burned hot and never cooled.

But Janice clutched the baby tighter. Where Laney saw burden, Janice saw power. For once, she wasn't the overlooked youngest or the cruel babysitter. With Crystal in her arms, she mattered. The lie made her important, the center of attention in a family that rarely looked her way.

She threw herself into the role completely. She rehearsed the story until it sounded natural, until the pauses and details matched. When anyone asked, she answered without hesitation. She dressed Crystal like her own, carried her proudly to family events, and corrected anyone who questioned it.

Even when a boyfriend claimed the baby was his, she never wavered. It wasn't loyalty or truth that held her; it was ownership. She's mine. All mine.

When Janice first held Crystal, she was only eighteen, newly back from Texas.

Yet there she was in posed photographs, smiling as if she had given birth herself. Pictures showed her holding the baby during visits, surrounded by family and friends in moments meant to feel celebratory. Others stood nearby, proud and unaware of what had already been set in motion.

The baby carrier sat ready, completing the illusion.

The pictures told one story, neat and believable.

The truth was far messier.

Janice had never been pregnant, and the family knew it.

Crystal, innocent in all of it, grew up calling Sandra "Aunt Sandy," never knowing "aunt" was the wrong word. The title itself was part of the cover, a layer of respectability over a dangerous truth.

Three years had passed since Barry began his affair with Halle, three years that Dorothy helped keep a secret.

She stood at the center of it all, not to save her son or protect his marriage, but to feed on the secrecy itself, taking quiet satisfaction in the pain, she unleashed within her own family.

## CHAPTER 17
# WHAT'S DONE IN THE DARK

What Barry tried to keep in the dark was bound to come into the light. Every secret waited to be exposed.

He crossed a line with an inappropriate workplace relationship involving his employee fifteen years younger and barely out of her teens. She was white. He was Black. The affair led to a pregnancy, and in 1980s New Jersey, intolerance left little room for an interracial relationship.

Instead of owning it, Barry enlisted his mother to conceal the truth, handing his youngest sister the role of raising his child so the baby wouldn't be placed in foster care.

Halle, the child's mother, was sent back to her racist mother's house, while Barry's marriage to Sandra stayed upright on the surface, appearing intact.

But lies don't stay buried. As the saying goes, 'oh, what a tangled web we weave when first we practice to deceive.'

His lies created traps that eventually began to close in around him. The web began to tighten because he was still obsessed with Halle, chasing in her the same sense of freedom he had once felt with Sandra.

You would think he learned his lesson after barely escaping the consequences of his actions, but he hadn't.

Yes, Barry was drawn back to her.

Halle had no intention of staying under her mother's roof. The racism was suffocating, a constant reminder of what she had given up. She found her own place, a small one-bedroom apartment with thin walls, a mattress on the floor, and a lock she controlled. It wasn't much, but it was hers.

That apartment became their meeting point. Recklessness turned into routine.

Halle's apartment strengthened the illusion. Their meetings took on a pattern, and their conversations turned toward a shared future. Barry promised that if she got her own place, he would leave Sandra and move in with her.

So, she did.

But Crystal had to be part of the plan. Halle knew that without the baby, she could never fully secure Barry's commitment.

Halle also knew she had never formally relinquished her parental rights. That knowledge gave her leverage and a way to strengthen her plan.

Dorothy had no paperwork, no custody order, no legal guardianship. In her attempt to protect her son, she gambled that Halle would fade away. What should have been secured with signatures and filings was left undone. That gap became decisive.

Janice refused to give Crystal up. Halle filed papers. Court was scheduled. The lines were drawn.

Barry could no longer keep his secret buried.

He chose a public dinner to confess, counting on Sandra's composure.

After the meal, Barry shifted uneasily and dropped his voice. "I have something to tell you."

His eyes stayed on the table. Then came the words he had carried like a stone for three years.

He confessed about the affair. He confessed about the baby. He admitted Janice had been raising Crystal for him.

He told her Halle wanted the child back and had taken the matter to court.

Every tangled thread spilled across the table, heavy and uninvited.

Sandra listened without interruption. To the room, she looked like a wife hearing an ordinary setback. Inside, she burned. Sixteen years of marriage had trained her to read the spaces between his sentences. She had long suspected his tie to Crystal ran deeper than he claimed. Now the truth had a docket number.

Divorce was not an option in her mind. She had given too much; her youth, her education, her fashion career, to the life they built.

To her, marriage was a covenant, not something to be broken by Barry's betrayal or another woman's intrusion. If she let it go now, she would lose more than a husband. She would lose the foundation she had fought to preserve for her children and herself.

She steadied her voice. She told Barry it would be all right. Outwardly, she made him feel safe, as though his confession hadn't destroyed her. Inwardly, she resolved that Halle would not take what she had protected for nearly two decades without a fight.

Barry claimed he still wanted the marriage, convincing himself they could endure. Sandra accepted his words, not out of belief but out of resolve. She wanted her marriage more than she trusted him. She declared she would stand with him in court, both to learn the full truth and to face the woman herself, making clear she wasn't going down without a fight.

But even in confession, Barry's lies lingered. He had just told Halle he would be with her. Now he told Sandra he wanted their marriage. His words to each woman contradicted one another, yet he spoke to them as if both could stand.

It was delusion or denial. Barry had lost contact with reality, convincing himself he could live in both worlds.

The courtroom would strip the illusion bare, exposing every secret he tried to hide.

## CHAPTER 18
# POETIC JUSTICE

The closer the court date came, the more desperate Barry became to control the outcome. His loyalties shifted with each conversation, leaning toward whoever held the most power at the time.

In the moment, Barry wasn't leaning on his mother to cover his tracks. He was now in partnership with Halle, a forbidden alliance that thrived on secrecy and betrayal. It was as if she had cast a spell on him, pulling him deeper into her world, blinding him to reason, responsibility, and family.

His confession at the dinner table had not come from courage but necessity.

When Barry told Janice that Halle wanted Crystal back, Janice refused. That refusal forced his hand.

And for Janice, it came out of nowhere.

Barry appeared at her door, his tone flat, his words sharp. "I came to take Crystal. Halle wants her back."

He broke her heart without hesitation or remorse.

Janice froze. "What are you talking about? No, you're not."

Barry stood firm. "She wants the baby. I'm taking her."

Janice's chest tightened. Crystal was asleep in the next room; her small body curled under the blanket.

"She's sleeping," Janice said, stepping into his path. "She doesn't know you. She doesn't know Halle. If you take her now, she'll wake up terrified."

Her voice shook with anger, but beneath it lay the cruel truth: she had no claim. For nearly two years, Crystal had been her daughter in every way that mattered, but there was no paperwork, no custody order, no protection.

"You lied," Janice told him. "You said she wasn't coming back. You knew I'd get attached."

Barry no longer moved like her brother. He wasn't himself. He acted as an instrument of Halle's will, carrying out her demand with the emptiness of a man under a spell.

The questions lingered in Janice's mind. Why now? Why, after all this time, did Halle suddenly want the child back? For nearly two years she had been absent and unconcerned.

Janice refused to hand Crystal over. If Halle wanted her, she would have to go to court.

If Janice wanted court, then court it would be. Halle had leverage and motivation. Having Crystal back would bind Barry to her in a way nothing else could.

And now the stakes were higher. Halle was pregnant again.

Another baby on the way made her determined to reclaim the first, using both children as leverage to tighten her hold on Barry and cement her place in his life.

On the morning of the hearing, Janice carried Crystal to the courthouse, dressed carefully, held tightly, as though she could hold back the tide. But at the courtroom door she was stopped. She could not enter.

The words landed like a blow. She obeyed, forced to hand Crystal over and wait in the hallway, listening to the echo of footsteps as the child she raised was led away.

Inside, the courtroom was cold. Halle sat at the plaintiff's table, her face steady, rehearsed. Dorothy sat across from her at the defendant's table, Barry sat in the gallery with Sandra at his side, the picture of unity.

The judge presiding over the case was brisk and unsparing.

From the start, the scales of justice were uneven. The contest was framed not as love versus abandonment but as a young white mother against the Black family who had taken in her child. Biology was weighed against devotion, and race hung over the room like a silent verdict. Halle's two years of absence were brushed aside.

The doctrine of unclean hands had to be acknowledged. The judge noted that while Halle had left Crystal with Janice, it was not done freely. It was under pressure and circumstances that could not be ignored. By law, the court could not reward deception or allow custody to rest on arrangements born of secrecy and bad faith.

But the absence of paperwork sealed the outcome. There was no custody agreement, no adoption, nothing binding to give Janice or Dorothy standing. The child's welfare was not the measure. The ruling was reduced to blunt simplicity: Halle was young, she was white, and she wanted her baby back.

The decision was swift and merciless. Crystal was to be returned to Halle immediately.

Waiting in the hallway, Janice was told she could go. There was no goodbye, no chance to explain. She walked out of the courthouse in disbelief, her arms empty, her heart broken.

She slid into the passenger seat of Dorothy's car. Dorothy gripped the wheel, eyes fixed straight ahead. Neither spoke.

The courthouse still clung to them, the echo of the gavel, the image of Crystal being led away, the cold finality of the order.

Then the radio betrayed them. Crystal's favorite song came

on, "I.O.U." by Freeze. The playful beat, the one built around those vowels Crystal used to sing at the top of her lungs, now cut like glass.

Janice broke. The song matched her grief, the melody hitting every place she was trying not to feel. Tears poured as she collapsed under the weight of her loss.

For Janice, the wound was unbearable. She carried it raw and permanently. She hated Halle.

As far as Janice was concerned, Halle didn't want or love her baby. She wanted her brother and used Crystal to get him.

That hatred burned sharper than grief because it was rooted not only in loss but in betrayal, the knowledge that love had never been the reason, only leverage.

Dorothy kept her hands steady, but her mind raced. She had thought she could shield her son, thought she could control the pieces. Instead, they shattered. And now, once again, she was behind the wheel at the moment of impact, not metal against metal, but truth against illusion.

Soon after the ruling, Barry had the audacity to make a request, proof of how selfish he and Halle really were.

He didn't ask himself; he knew better than to face Janice directly. He sent Dorothy.

His mother would always do what he asked.

The weight of Dorothy's responsibility for Crystal, and the part she played in creating the situation, pressed down on her. Despite Barry and Halle's egregious actions, she felt compelled to step in once more, convinced that advocating for the child was the only way to make sense of the damage left behind.

She carried the request to Janice on his behalf: Would she come into Halle's home to help Crystal adjust?

Dorothy's words carried their own heaviness. She had been part of the machinery that kept Barry's secret alive, helping to build the very chaos that had destroyed them. Now she had to face the consequences, to witness Crystal's pain, her cries, her fear, and the heartbreak Dorothy had helped create.

The irony was that they were all guilty, all accomplices in one way or another. As cruel as it was, as devastating as it felt, neither Janice nor Dorothy could step away from the situation now.

Were they victims? Absolutely not. The entire effort had been about saving Barry's marriage and keeping his family intact.

Crystal was the true victim, caught in the wreckage of their deceit. So were Sandra, Adrienne, Barry Jr., Carlos, and Sonny, all of them forced to live with the fallout.

But none of them cared. Their focus stayed on themselves, on protecting what little control they still believed they had.

When Janice agreed, it was only for Crystal. Never for Barry. Never for Halle.

She walked into that house and the air felt wrong, thick with what had been taken. Crystal stood in front of the television. When she saw Janice, she spun in a circle, clapping, and rushed into her arms, squealing, "Mommy!"

She held tight, burying her face in Janice's chest as if she had finally come home.

Janice's heart broke. She forced the correction through trembling lips. "No, baby. I'm Aunt Janice."

But Crystal shook her head. Not even two years old, she was certain. "No. Mommy."

Halle saw it, the way the child clung, the way the word came out naturally, as if she always belonged to Janice.

Halle winced at the sound of Crystal calling Janice Mommy.

Maybe in that moment, all of Halle's buried regrets surfaced, twisting into jealousy toward Janice and quiet disdain for Crystal. It tightened her jaw. She tried to mask it with a smile, but the truth was plain.

Crystal didn't know her, didn't want her, didn't reach for her. The reality of what Halle had done was beginning to take shape.

Perhaps she never wanted Janice's help at all. Maybe Barry insisted, hoping to smooth things over, forcing Halle to accept a woman whose presence reminded her of the damage she had caused.

Maybe in Halle's mind, Janice wasn't helping. Maybe she felt like Janice was in the way, prolonging a bond that should have been broken. Halle might have dismissed it coldly, insisting Crystal would "get used to it," as if motherhood could be claimed by decree rather than earned through love.

Every interaction between Janice and Crystal could've reminded Halle of what she could never replace. The bond between them was natural, unforced, and painfully visible.

For eight weeks, Janice stayed in that house. Because in all the chaos, Crystal still wanted her, still clung to her, still called her Mommy.

And throughout her stay, Janice lived the contradiction. She was a mother in the child's eyes and a servant in everyone else's.

## CHAPTER 19
# STRANGER IN MY HOUSE

After court, Barry returned home to Sandra under the pretense of reconciliation. His mind was fractured and his reality distorted.

Still drawn to Halle, Barry turned the tables on Sandra.

After everything, he claimed he was unhappy in the marriage. He convinced himself the excuse would make him appear justified instead of guilty.

He attacked Sandra's dream of working in real estate, twisting her ambition into a flaw. Every flyer she designed, every open house she prepared, every hour she invested, he dismissed as foolish. He mocked her expenses, pointing out that she hadn't sold a single house, as if that erased her effort.

The irony was harsh.

Sandra had once been accepted into the Fashion Institute of Technology, one of the top fashion schools in the world. She had the talent to build a career in design but gave it up to marry Barry, to follow him through military bases, to raise their children, and to support his ambitions. She carried his name, his household, and his stability. In return, he tore down her attempt at independence.

Behind his criticism was the truth: Barry wanted the freedom to chase a young white woman, and he was willing to blame Sandra to get it.

He picked a fight with her and moved in with Halle.

Within a week, the illusion with Halle collapsed. Barry was a grown man sleeping on a mattress on the floor of a one-bedroom apartment, his frightened child and youngest sister curled on the sofa. It was a picture of failure.

In a moment of clarity, he went back home. Sandra opened the door in silence and let him in.

But for her, the truth had already arrived. The man she had loved since high school was gone.

She studied him carefully, realizing how far he had drifted. The warmth that once filled their home had turned cold. The tenderness that once defined their marriage had hardened into distance. His touch, his tone, the way he looked at her no longer belonged to the man she had fallen in love with. The version of Barry standing before her was a stranger wearing a familiar face.

He would not stay long. Fate, or a promise from the past, saw to that.

Two years earlier, during their first confrontation, Halle's sister had leaned in, eyes sharp, and asked Barry what his intentions were. He stumbled, but Halle was defiant: she was keeping the baby. Her sister made a promise Barry couldn't ignore. If he tried to walk away, someone would hurt him.

Now that promise matured into consequence. Words became action. Men showed up at the house.

One afternoon, Sandra rounded the side of the house on her way to her car. Two men had Barry pinned against the siding. Startled, she asked if everything was all right. Barry brushed her off quickly. "Yes. Go ahead and run your errand."

When she returned, Barry announced he was leaving.

She didn't resist. She knew he was no longer the man she once loved. He was already gone. But unlike the others, she refused to do his dirty work for him. If he was leaving, he would face the children himself, like the man he was supposed to be.

Barry gathered them in the bedroom: Adrienne, fourteen; her brothers, ten and five; and their cousin Sonny, about sixteen. In a flat, matter-of-fact tone, he announced he was leaving.

No reason. No explanation. No attempt to connect his decision to the wreckage he had created. He didn't say divorce. He didn't admit weakness. He simply said he was going.

His voice was heavy, a baritone so deep it seemed to rattle the walls. He never needed to yell; the weight of his tone punished on its own.

So, when he turned to Sonny and asked if he wanted to come with him, it didn't sound like an invitation. It sounded like a command.

Sonny's fear was plain, shoulders tight, eyes darting, body shrinking under that voice. But then something shifted. Against the pressure, against the fear, he said, "No." Quiet, but firm. He chose to stay. A boy's defiance rang louder than Barry's authority.

That was what cut the deepest. Not that he was leaving, but that in the moment of collapse he reached for Sonny, trying to pull him from the wreckage while leaving his own children behind. Adrienne and her brothers weren't offered a hand. They weren't given a choice. They were simply abandoned.

Sonny refused the hand. He chose the battered stability of

their broken home over the uncertainty of following a man already halfway gone.

And then Barry left.

Not in spectacle, not in noise, just in disappearance. No zipper tugged, no suitcase carried, no door creaked open or shut. He didn't walk out. He slipped away, like Houdini pulling his coldest trick, erasing himself from the room.

His departure felt like another hit and run, sudden and crushing. At the scene, Sandra gathered them. Bruised and bleeding herself, she found the strength to pull them from the debris. With shaking hands and a battered spirit, she lifted Adrienne, her brothers, and Sonny from the wreckage Barry left behind. She tended to their wounds even as her own went untreated.

In that moment, Sandra decided. Barry had offered Sonny a conditional escape: come with me, leave them behind. Sandra gave him something different: unconditional belonging. It didn't matter that Sonny was Franny's child. She claimed him as her own. She raised him as her son, not with secrecy or shame, but with love.

Sandra refused to collapse. She could have sunk into despair and left the children to fend for themselves.

Instead, she hid her tears, contained her anger, and never let them see her crack. She didn't curse Barry. She didn't accuse him. She didn't burden the children with blame. She told them simply that this was his decision, and she left the rest unsaid.

Inside, she was in shock. Her sixteen-year marriage was destroyed. She was left with four mouths to feed and no clear path.

So, she got in the car, angry and disoriented, and drove south on the New Jersey Turnpike, past concrete stretches and toll booths, across the Delaware Memorial Bridge where steel towers rose like gates. She stayed on Interstate 95, mile after mile, not stopping once, not even at the Maryland House.

Hours later she realized how far she had gone. She found herself on the Baltimore-Washington Parkway, pulling off at the Laurel exit, in Maryland, where her older sister Pat lived.

Pat was a woman of God, and Sandra knew if she reached her, Pat would pray in a way no one else could, pouring strength back into her, enough to turn the car around and face her reality with pride and dignity.

## CHAPTER 20
# HOUSE OF CARDS

**B**arry gambled his marriage, his children, and his stability on Halle, convinced the bet would deliver a new life. But the prize he imagined never arrived.

Not long after Barry left Sandra and the children, Halle gave birth to their second child. Maybe this second pregnancy was the moment everything shifted for her. What had started as an affair now carried permanence.

Two children tied her to Barry in ways that passion alone never could.

Perhaps in Halle's mind, the birth changed her status. She no longer wanted to be the hidden woman or the whispered name in someone else's story. She wanted Barry completely, his name, his loyalty, his future.

The second child might have felt like her claim, proof that what they shared was real and deserved recognition.

Maybe that was what pushed her toward court. The secrecy had worn thin, and she wanted to force the truth into the open, to make official what she believed was already hers.

What she did not see was that their relationship had been

doomed from the start. Anything built on secrecy and betrayal could never grow into trust.

A house raised on sand will sink, and theirs was weaker still, a house of cards fragile against the first strong gust.

Barry mistook escape for freedom and desire for love. What he and Halle had was never meant to stand.

She would not become his wife until 1986, and in those two years before marriage no foundation was laid, no future built. After all, Barry was still married to Sandra when the second child was born and was not granted a divorce until 1985.

There were no dreams shaped together, only arguments that chipped at the walls, disillusionment that hollowed out the rooms, and decay spreading through every corner.

What should have been a home was instead a structure waiting for collapse, cursed to fall under the weight of the choices that built it.

The cracks showed first in Halle's treatment of Crystal. She never bonded with her, never made the connection.

Janice hovered close, uneasy, watching with mistrust. Crystal struggled under the strain of it all, made worse when the new baby girl arrived.

Janice took on the work Halle refused: potty training, nurturing, standing in the gap with love where Halle left a void.

Halle poured herself into the younger child, indulging her every want, while Crystal bore rejection. When the younger girl complained that her hair wasn't long enough, Halle took scissors to Crystal's head, cutting it near bald so she wouldn't outshine her sister.

Janice warned that Halle was both mentally and physically abusive. But when child protective services arrived, the scales tipped. The word of the young white mother outweighed the

Black surrogate raising alarms. The system believed Halle and dismissed Janice.

As the second child grew, Janice could no longer stomach what she saw. She stepped back, leaving Crystal more vulnerable than ever.

More than once, Barry had to stand between Halle and his daughter when cruelty turned physical, with Halle striking Crystal across the face.

Two years later, they welcomed a third child, a son. But the addition of another child did not mend the cracks.

It only added weight to a house already leaning, a tower built too high on lies and deceit.

Barry's frustrations spilled into anger, lashing out at anyone within reach. After a tense exchange with Sandra over seeing the children, he carried his fury into the car.

Dina sat in the back seat, Barry driving, Halle beside him. Sharp-eyed and unwilling to stay silent, Dina leaned forward and cut him with the truth, "What do you expect after how you and Halle have treated her?"

The words pierced him, a mirror he refused to face. His reaction was instant, not thought through.

He hauled off and slapped Dina so hard the sound cracked through the car, shocking even Halle.

Barry's rage erupted, startling Halle into defense. His violence was a flashback to the moment years earlier when he was ordered to discipline Dina as a child. The same anger resurfaced, alive and unchecked, shaking the fragile walls of their home.

Marriage to Halle did not steady the structure. Prejudice was another card stacked into the fragile frame, alive in her mother's hatred for Black people. It showed itself most clearly when Barry's children came to visit.

Sandra never stood in their way, but she would not force them either.

At Halle's mother's house, the disdain could not be hidden.

Adrienne and her brothers were kept outside, refused entry as if their presence threatened the walls. They waited in the backyard, treated like field slaves not welcome in Massa's house.

Adrienne was old enough to see it, old enough to name the insult.

Refusing to accept mistreatment as the price of seeing her father, she ended the visits.

Another card slipped from the fragile tower, leaving Barry with less than he had bargained for, trapped in the shadow of the life he had chosen.

As cards kept falling, Dorothy, through sleight of hand, kept gathering them back into the deck, hiding Barry's losses. She shielded him quietly, guarding him from the wreckage he created.

When Adrienne and her brothers went weeks without hearing from their father, she would call Dorothy, searching for answers. Dorothy, with practiced lies, always claimed ignorance.

Yet within the hour Barry's voice would appear on the line, pretending he was simply checking in.

To the children, it felt like a rigged game; his moves hidden, Dorothy holding his whereabouts close to the chest.

The cold visits to Halle's house and the wall of lies built by Dorothy fractured Adrienne's bond with her father until it finally broke.

For five years she spoke not a word to him. The closeness they once shared, the daughter who adored her father, was shattered, buried under absence, betrayal, and silence.

Adrienne's refusal to speak was the truest measure of

collapse, an empty space where a father's voice no longer reached.

It was Halle's idea to move, once again steering Barry's course.

The relocation to Virginia was not chance but design, her way of cutting him off further from his family and children and tightening her grip.

But the move did not strengthen their marriage. There was nothing solid to hold. Their life together was not built on love but on lies, not on trust but on deceit.

In Virginia, without family nearby to witness, protect, and coverup, infidelity marked both sides of the union.

Each betrayal fed the other until fidelity was no longer even expected.

Barry and Halle circled one another like opponents in the same ring, both throwing blows, both keeping score.

The affairs were not secrets but weapons, each one proof that the relationship had become little more than a contest of power. Where trust should have lived, suspicion sat heavy. Where hope might have grown, resentment spread.

Barry traded stability for the dream of freedom, but what he found was a prison with mirrored walls. Halle, who once craved the title of wife, found little satisfaction in its reality. Instead of a home, they built a battleground.

The unraveling was inevitable. Arguments grew sharper, silences longer. What little connection remained was consumed by bitterness and betrayal.

In the end, there was no storm or collapse, only the steady erosion of a structure that had no foundation. Their marriage did not explode; it decayed. Piece by piece, lie by lie, until nothing bound them but memory and regret.

By the early 1990s Barry was holding less than he had when he left New Jersey; failing marriage, no peace, and a distance from his older three children that could not be mended.

Halle was left with the hollow prize she fought for, a title without love, a house without trust.

Janice and Dorothy followed them south. Dorothy would not cut the tether to her son, and Janice needed to be close to watch over Crystal even from the outside. Wherever Barry went, the women who enabled his choices were never far behind.

Barry sought refuge not at home but on the road. To escape the reality, he created and the psychosis that haunted him, he turned to trucking, staying gone for weeks at a time. The miles became his cover, the drone of the engine a barrier against the chaos he had unleashed. Yet every hour on the highway was not freedom but avoidance.

His heart, hardened from years of misdeeds, betrayed him at last. On the very roads he used for escape, his heart failed.

In 1993, he was admitted to Sentara Heart Hospital in Norfolk, Virginia, where doctors implanted a left ventricular assist device (LVAD), a machine to keep him alive until a new heart could be found.

The heart that came, a younger, stronger, kinder heart, entered his chest and, symbolically, his story.

The transplant marked the end of one life and the beginning of another. Not long after receiving this new heart, his relationship with Halle collapsed for good.

Barry returned to where he had started, under the same roof as Dorothy and Janice. He was given another chance to reclaim his life, but he remained tethered to the wreckage of his choices.

## CHAPTER 21
# MY SISTER'S STORY

When Barry left Halle, the house did not lose only a husband. It lost its last illusion of control. But the damage had started long before he walked out.

Crystal's life was built on deception from her first breath. She was the product of a bargain struck in secrecy and shame, conceived in betrayal and passed like property between women who mistook manipulation for love.

Her birth was a transaction: Halle using a child to secure a man, Barry using desire to escape his life, and Dorothy using her daughter Janice to protect her one son. And Janice caught up in the lie by circumstance.

No one told the truth, not then and not for years.

Dorothy built her world around Barry. Every secret she kept, every lie she told, was meant to shield him. She called it love, but it was worship, the kind that blinds a mother to her child's misdeeds.

Janice became her instrument, carrying out orders that kept Dorothy's hands clean and Barry's reputation intact. It was the beginning of a family tradition: women sacrificing truth to preserve the one son.

Barry and Halle's relationship was built on performance, his charm and her longing, pretending to be love.

What began as seduction became dependency. By the time Crystal arrived, the affair had hardened into obligation. Halle believed the baby would bind them together. Barry believed he could manage both worlds.

Both were wrong.

When Barry finally left, the illusion collapsed. The promise of love turned to resentment, and the little girl born to hold a man became the reminder of everything broken.

Though he was free of Halle, he left behind the child he once fought to keep from "the system." Crystal did not escape a system; she entered a different one: one of control, punishment, and denial.

Later came the unthinkable: sexual abuse by Halle's longtime boyfriend.

Crystal told her mother what was happening. Halle refused to believe her. The man disguised as a mentor was a predator, creeping into Crystal's room at night.

In desperation, Crystal ran to Dorothy and Janice for safety. She didn't have the words to articulate what was happening to her, although she tried. Each time, Halle would call, demanding her return, and they complied.

Once again, the white mother was trusted over the Black daughter. Even Barry, unaware or unwilling to see, sent her back to the house she feared most.

Crystal would one day tell her own story, the story of cruelty endured while no one believed her. The story of a girl who ran for safety and was punished for running. Freedom came only when she was old enough to emancipate herself, walking away from the wreckage of the house of cards.

She often wondered what other people learned first from their parents. How to love without fear. How to rest without worry. How to recognize love when it entered the room.

She was the eldest of three in the house that Barry and Halle built, a house that looked whole from the outside but swayed within, a fragile structure balanced on silence. Love was scarce. Affection foreign. No hugs. No gentle words. Only the tension of people pretending not to break.

The memories of her childhood felt like a sprint through falling walls, breathless and relentless, the finish line always out of reach. In her mind, the starter pistol still fires. On your mark. The gun cracks. She runs, heart pounding, lungs burning, chasing a peace that never stayed.

People asked, "What are you running from?" She said nothing. She wanted to believe it. But the truth was simpler. She wasn't running away. She was running to get out of the way before the house of cards could bury her.

Years later, in quiet moments, she would return there, in dreams, in sounds, in the stillness between breaths.

The walls were always the same color. The air still carried the weight of what was never said. Sometimes she heard her younger self calling out, still waiting for help that never came.

Her childhood came back in fragments. She kept the worst locked away. What remained said enough. She felt unloved and unwanted at home. She looked for love where she could find it, often where she should not. She was sexually abused for years. Rage seeped in.

Moodiness, insecurity, a hollow center. She tried to outrun it, but the past kept pace.

Adulthood brought collisions, failed relationships, strained friendships, and distance from family. She avoided confrontation, then avoided people altogether. If she did not cut you off, she absorbed too much and smiled through it. She gave endless chances and blamed herself for the harm done by others. She could not yet see the pattern; you teach people how to treat you.

Trust thinned until it was gone. Alone felt easier. She wore calm like armor. People asked, "Does anything bother you?" She said, "I'm fine." They told her to smile. She refused the performance. Numbness settled in.

The break began in 2020.

On Facebook, she followed an empath who read people's energy. His words moved differently, calm, steady, certain. She booked a session, unsure why, only knowing she was drawn to the light in his voice.

An empath, she learned, was someone who feels what others feel, who carries the energy of the room in their own body. They do not just sense emotion; they absorb it. To some, it is intuition. To others, it is a gift, one that can heal if used with care.

When the session began, he closed his eyes and breathed deeply. "Crystal," he said softly, "this is not you. You're carrying what isn't yours. You need to heal."

She'd heard similar words before, but never like this. Something in his tone cut through her defenses. She was tired of being broken. This time, she listened.

She began with what felt simple, removing what dimmed her light. People. Habits. Rooms where the air felt wrong. Each decision was a small act of self-respect.

She learned that healing is energetic work. Some spirits drain you. Others restore you.

To rise, she had to choose peace over attachment, even when peace meant being alone. Family, too, could carry the wrong energy, and she released them with love.

That summer, she took a course and became a certified mental health coach. The lessons opened her eyes to the power of vibration and truth. Helping others heal began to heal her. For the first time, she understood that pain, when faced, transforms into purpose.

For years, her substitute for therapy had been Iyanla, Fix My Life.

She watched, took notes, and whispered answers meant for someone else. Friends offered advice that felt good in the moment but did not last.

Then Adrienne told her, "You need professional help."

She resisted. "I'm not crazy," she said. But she went anyway.

Counseling met her where she was. Her therapist listened with grace and spoke with clarity.

In those sessions, Crystal learned that her empathy, what she once thought was weakness, was her power. She discovered how easily she absorbed the pain of others, confusing it for love. She traced that instinct back to childhood, to the house that taught her to carry other people's weight.

Healing was not pretty. It rarely is. Pain lingers until it is named. She forgave herself first, the hardest and most necessary step. She said it aloud: "I forgive you for carrying pain that was never yours. I forgive you for trying to earn love from those who could not give it."

Then she began forgiving the rest, not because they deserved it, but because she deserved freedom.

Each release felt like an exhale after years of holding her breath. The energy shifted. Her spirit lightened. The work had begun to do what time alone could not.

Part of Crystal's healing came through words. She joined a writing project where women told their stories, the pain, the survival, the reckoning. Each page became a prayer. They wrote about what had been done to them, how they endured, how they coped, and finally, how they forgave.

They forgave the ones who caused the harm.

They forgave the ones who stood by and did nothing.

They forgave themselves for carrying the blame.

Writing became ritual. Every sentence was a release, every paragraph a cleansing. Putting her pain on paper turned memory into meaning.

The truth cost her what little remained of her relationship with Halle.

That bond had always been fragile, built on silence and performance.

When truth arrived, it burned through them both. Crystal learned that sometimes it is better not to have a mother than to pretend you share one.

Halle could not face what Crystal had survived under her roof. She could not bear to look at the daughter who refused to carry her shame. Their distance was the final evidence of the same denial that began with Dorothy and the One Son.

But where Halle turned away, Crystal turned inward. She faced what others buried. She chose truth over image, honesty over silence.

Her healing was not about repairing what was lost with Halle. It was about breaking free from the inheritance of denial, the need to protect men, to excuse harm, to swallow pain for peace.

When Crystal said I forgive you, it was not to invite her mother back. It was to free herself from the story she was born into. Forgiveness became her liberation. Healing became her legacy.

For the first time in this family's long and tangled history, a daughter refused to repeat the pattern.

What began in deceit ended in deliverance because she chose herself.

And though Halle could never love her the way she needed, Crystal learned to love herself in ways her mother never could.

That was the true ending of their mother-daughter story, the one Halle could not admit, but Crystal could finally tell.

Crystal's truth lived in the shadows of Barry's choices, but life went on in the house he left behind.

While one home crumbled under the weight of deceit, another stood firm through faith, order, and endurance.

Sandra had no time for the ruins Barry made elsewhere. Her hands were full holding up what remained.

## CHAPTER 22
# HOUSE PARTY

Barry left his world of stability to step into the world of uncertainty and risk, collapsing under the weight of deceit.

Sandra built the world she created; intentional, structured, grounded in both love and discipline.

The Avenue held birthdays and cookouts, fun and games on the back deck, the sound of laughter spilling into the street. It became the gathering place, for Sandra's and Barry's family alike, where loyalty and love outweighed whatever division, the adults had caused.

Barry's family seemed to belong more to Sandra than to him. When he moved to Virginia, it was as if he had exiled himself. The center of gravity shifted. The Avenue was no longer just an address; it was the family's foundation.

Through it all, Sandra and Dina remained close. Dina saw Sandra as her big sister, someone she could lean on when life grew heavy. If she needed encouragement, a quick getaway, or a safe place to send her children for the summer, Sandra always said yes. Their bond never wavered, proof that Sandra's role in the family reached far beyond her own household.

In the end, that was Sandra's gift. Her love bound people together in ways that outlasted betrayal, distance, and even time.

The Avenue was the witness.

That same spirit extended to Janice. Despite everything that unfolded, Sandra kept the door open. At a family gathering, she pulled Janice aside, motioned for her to sit, and asked about Crystal.

The room buzzed with chatter, but between them the air was heavy with silence. Janice's heart pounded. For years she'd dreaded this moment, fearing Sandra's anger. She had been only eighteen, swept up in decisions bigger than her, but fear does not yield to reason. She expected judgment, maybe even rejection.

Instead, Sandra released her from it. She told Janice she wasn't angry with her. The blame rested squarely on the adults. The words gave Janice a relief she hadn't known she needed. Where she expected condemnation, she received understanding.

Sandra was honest though. The wound was real. For two years she believed Crystal was her niece.

Discovering the truth left her deeply disappointed. Betrayal never lost its sting. Yet even in her pain, Sandra made a choice. She refused to let bitterness define her. She would not pass her hurt onto the children, or onto a young woman who had been little more than a child herself.

Sandra gathered her family and made her expectations plain. No one was to speak badly about Barry in front of the children. She would not allow their father's failures to become poison poured into their young souls.

If bitterness lived in her, she buried it. If anger rose, she silenced it.

Whatever feelings Adrienne, Barry Jr., Carlos, and Sonny came to hold about their father, Sandra insisted, would come directly from Barry's actions, not from her words or her family's contempt.

Her children would come to their own truths in their own time, by their father's presence or his absence.

It was the discipline of love and a shield of protection. Sandra knew children carried their parents' wounds like invisible scars, and she refused to deepen them.

That moment revealed Sandra's strength in its purest form. She could carry disappointment without turning it into punishment. She could acknowledge betrayal without letting it poison her home.

The children saw this. Every child who came through her doors felt it.

The Bradleys, the Littles, the Macks, the Rosses, the Scotts, the Thomases, the Woodses and all their friends knew Aunt Sandy's house was a place of love.

Even Halle's children, who sometimes crossed her doorstep, were welcomed. They too called her Aunt Sandra.

It was a sharp contrast to the way Adrienne and her brothers were treated at Halle's mother's house, where disdain was never hidden and prejudice cut cold.

Sandra's house was more than a home. It was a promise that no matter what the adults did, the children would always have a place where they belonged.

Every neighborhood child who crossed her threshold carried away the same lesson: Ms. Woods' house was safe, but it came with rules. And if you broke them, she'd make sure your parents knew.

So, when Adrienne, Kym, LaQuita and Tonya thought they

were slick skipping school to spend the day in downtown Newark, their plan fell apart quickly. Not only did the school call, but the girls also showed up on a news segment set to air that evening.

Sandra didn't wait; she picked up the phone and called every mother. By the time the girls walked through the door, the story had already beaten them home.

Sandra's house absorbed it all the music, the quarrels, the reconciliations, and gave back a sense of belonging no one else could offer.

Sandra loved a good party, especially a birthday. Not just the day. The whole season of it.

Her birthday lasted all of February. Anyone who called the house heard it right away. If you were not calling to wish her a happy birthday, she would call you back in March.

She loved birthday traditions too. The laughter. The little rituals. And the saying that always came with it. A lick and a pinch so you don't get sick. It was delivered with playful taps, teasing smiles, and the kind of affection that made birthdays feel earned.

She was not a poet or a rapper, but she loved making up birthday songs anyway. Little rhymes, made up on the spot for whoever she was calling. No two were the same. Some were clever. Some barely made sense. All of them said the same thing. You mattered enough to get your own song.

Summer birthdays were her favorite, especially August and September. They gave her a reason to throw the annual cookout. She combined everything she could. August and September birthdays. End of summer. Back to school. Labor Day. One party with many reasons, all of them joyful.

She squeezed every name she could onto the cake. Adrienne. Kevin. George. Sonny. Rashaan. And whoever else came to mind. The letters crowded the frosting, looping and bumping into one another. That was the point. If you were there, you belonged on the cake.

For Sandra, parties were never just parties. They were how she marked time. How she gathered people. How she reminded everyone that joy was still possible, even when life said otherwise. Celebration was not a break from responsibility for her. It was how she held things together.

Sandra carried that same energy into the new year. New Year's Day was not just a date on the calendar. It was an event, and it started with rules.

Before the year could turn, the house had to be cleaned from top to bottom. No shortcuts. No corners missed. There could not be a single dirty piece of clothing left in a hamper. Sandra believed you did not walk into a new year with old mess. A clean house and clean clothes set the tone for what was coming.

New Year's Eve came with one more requirement. Before the kids were allowed to go out with their friends, they had to help clean the chitlins. Chitterlings. Pig intestines that had to be scrubbed, trimmed, and rinsed again and again before they ever saw a pot. It was work, and it was intentional. Sandra only cooked them once a year, for her New Year's Day open house.

Adrienne hated everything about them. The smell. The cleaning. The taste. Sandra knew it and did not care.

"They aren't for you," she would say. "Clean them anyway."

By New Year's Day, the house was ready. The food was hot. The door stayed open. Anyone could stop by for a plate and a Happy New Year toast. Family. Neighbors. Friends of friends. Sandra welcomed them all.

That was her way. You started the year clean, fed, and surrounded by people. And if you walked through her door on New Year's Day, you left full, whether you planned to or not.

# THE ONE SON

Sandra created spaces where Adrienne, Barry Jr., Carlos, and Sonny could laugh, dance, and feel safe.

The gatherings on the Avenue proved it: in Sandra's house, life wasn't crumbling, it was alive with music, community, and hope.

On the Avenue she carved out joy, holding the family together. When she opened her doors, the block came alive.

The Field was where the kids ran free. The basement was where Sandra set the tone. Music pounding. Kids packed shoulder to shoulder. Laughter rising through the concrete floor. She turned survival into celebration, and the house itself became the party.

And those parties were legendary.

Flyers Adrienne and Sonny printed themselves promised the night, and kids from all over Tinton Falls and Red Bank showed up.

Sandra allowed it, but she took her cut. After all, it was her basement.

Sonny kept the turntables thumping until the walls sweated, while Adrienne and her friends hustled sodas from behind the bar like it was their own club.

The heat. The noise. The joy of young bodies. Those nights felt bigger than their block, bigger than the Fruit Bowl itself.

The basement would turn into a hot, sticky sauna, the kind of night you could not miss. If you did, you would hear about it for weeks.

And when the crowd grew too big and spilled into the backyard, their grumpy neighbor Mr. Peppe was guaranteed to call the police. He hated the noise and loved nothing more than making them pay. He was notorious for confiscating her brothers' basketballs when they bounced into his yard. He was the perfect neighbor.

Still, Sandra let the parties run late. Midnight. Sometimes

one in the morning. Until she would swing open the basement door and flash the lights. That was the warning. If people did not clear out, she came down herself, and no one wanted to test her. She was straight out of Brick City, and everybody knew she would throw hands if she had to.

But here is the truth. People did not love Sandra because they feared her. They loved her because she loved them. Her door was always open. If a neighbor needed sugar, flour, or a ride, she was there. If a kid needed a plate of food, she fed them. If someone needed a couch, she made space.

Everybody on the Avenue and beyond knew her and respected her, not because she demanded it, but because she gave so much of herself.

## CHAPTER 23
# THE CRAZIES

Sandra cared for more than her own children. People respected her authority. She was the steady hand, the open door, the voice people trusted.

The care and the crazy showed up in every corner of the house, animals included.

His name was Felipe.

Sandra named him thinking he was a French poodle, unaware the breed actually originated in Germany and was only later associated with France through style and grooming.

She chose the name Felipe believing it was French as well, not knowing it was Spanish and Portuguese instead.

It didn't matter. A German dog with a not-quite-right French name felt fitting for Sandra, shaped by her time overseas and a life that never stayed neatly in one place.

Felipe was part of the crazy. A black poodle with his tail left long because Sandra saw no reason to cut away what God had given him. No one walked him. No one worried much about where he went.

Smart and self-possessed, he held his own in the Woods house, on the Avenue, and throughout the Fruit Bowl.

Felipe roamed like he belonged to the town itself, slipping through backyards, crossing streets with purpose, turning up wherever the day carried him. Friends would casually report sightings. They'd seen Felipe at the Field. They'd seen him trotting down the Avenue like he had somewhere important to be.

He lived as freely as the family did, uncontained but not lost. By nightfall, he always found his way home.

Felipe wasn't the only one who came and went that way. The house had a way of taking in transients.

After Barry left, she still had four mouths to feed, three of them teenage boys, and that's when the boarders came. She offered a room and regular meals in exchange for monthly rent.

The kids called them "The Crazies" because each had something off: missing teeth, odd habits, strange ways of moving through the world.

Some young, some old. Men and women. Most had no family, or worse, family who didn't want them.

Sometimes relatives checked in. Others were dropped off and forgotten, like the old lady they called Ms. Anne.

The word was she'd been mean as hell in her prime, and by the time she got old, no one claimed her.

The kids laughed because she never got their names right and called everybody a girl.

"Hey Angie, Barbara, Carla, Stacey!" she'd shout from her room.

They'd play dumb, then laugh in the hallway. She'd sit on a high-back chair like a throne, facing the hall, waiting to catch someone walking by.

They griped until one day; Sandra's mother heard it and shut it down.

"Be blessed to live as long as Ms. Anne," she told them.

# THE ONE SON

"Don't complain about helping an old woman. Pray you make it to her age, and somebody cares enough to help you when you do."

The boarders tested everyone, but no one more than Sandra. One summer day, she showed the block exactly what "Brick City" looked like, the day she fought one of the Crazies in the front yard.

Stephanie was her name. She had a seven-year-old daughter rumored to be Sonny's older brother Mark's child. Stephanie picked the wrong day. She was upset over some grievance and decided to voice her complaint while Sandra was entertaining a real-estate client in the living room and about to go show properties.

Sandra brushed her off and headed to the car. Stephanie followed, banging on the window.

That was it. Earrings off. Car door swung open. Sandra beat her down in the front yard. Kids came running, chanting, "Go, Ms. Woods! Get her!" like a title bout.

Adrienne was mortified, yelling for Sonny to break it up. He tried and got tossed like a rag doll.

By the time the police rolled up, Sandra declared, "Pack your shit in a trash bag and be out of my house before I get back or I'll beat your ass again." Then she drove off with her client like nothing happened.

When she returned, the boarder and her daughter were gone.

That was Sandra, fierce and unapologetic.

She didn't care how tall or tough the boys got. If they crossed a line, she would pin them to the wall and remind them whose house it was.

Her warnings weren't idle. Test her and she would, "smack the taste out your mouth."

Her punishments were calculated. Spankings took energy,

and she hated wasting it. If it came to that, a line had been crossed that couldn't be erased.

Hanging on the side of the kitchen cabinet was her weapon of choice: a battered wooden paddle. In faded letters it read, 'The Fanny Whacker! A Spanking Good Idea!' Beneath it, a list of "reasons to use it," both decoration and warning.

If one of the kids acted up after she'd worked all day, the process was fixed.

First, the psychological: "Go to your room and wait for me." The waiting dragged on, an hour, sometimes more, long enough to hope she'd forgotten. She never forgot.

Second, the physical. She appeared in the doorway, paddle in hand. "Pull down your pants and get across my lap." No chasing. Efficiency mattered. Whacks matched years: ten years old, ten whacks; eight years old, eight whacks. Precise.

Then the emotional reset. Pants back up. Arms around them. "You know mommy loves you."

The hug at the end was the worst part. They wanted to stay mad but needed the hug in that moment.

She didn't play in public either. Before leaving for the store, she lined them up. "Let me give each of you a slap on the behind now, so you don't act up when we get there."

School was nonnegotiable. Attendance wasn't a choice. It was expected. Aim for perfect.

Sick? The child didn't decide. The doctor did. Stomachache, doctor. Fever, doctor. Whatever it was, a professional ruled. If the verdict was fit for school, she'd drop you off after the appointment.

No mental-health days. No "I don't feel like it." In Sandra's house, school was mandatory.

She was consistent. Equal opportunist. No "boy chores" or "girl chores."

Everybody cooked. Everybody cleaned. Everybody washed dishes.

Everybody took out the trash. Skip your turn and you paid. If the bathroom wasn't clean, she dumped Ajax in the tub and left it there until someone scrubbed it spotless.

Every morning started at the refrigerator. The chore list hung there, assignments in her handwriting, half the words misspelled, none of the meaning lost. The kids would chuckle, then she'd cut it off: "You knew damn well what I meant."

She was hands-on. If something broke, she fixed it.

Even cars. She'd pile the kids into the car and head to the Craft Shop at Fort Monmouth, the "Do It Yourself" garage. Oil changes. Filters. Spark plugs. Knowing how wasn't required. Trying was.

The yard was no exception. Everyone shoveled snow, raked leaves, clipped hedges.

Saturday mornings, if friends showed up to hang, she didn't excuse the kids. She handed out rakes and trash bags. If you were in her yard, you were part of the work.

The only exception was after Barry Jr.'s accident. It was his turn to cut the grass. A stick jammed the mower. He pulled it free. With no automatic shut-off, the blade kicked and sheared two fingers.

He was in the front yard when it happened, but shock sent him running around the house through the back door, bloody and screaming. Adrienne was at the sink. Sandra and her mother Mary were at the kitchen table.

Chaos ensued.

In a blur, they wrapped his hand and threw him in the back seat of the car. No ambulance, just straight to the hospital.

Minutes later, the phone rang. Sandra's voice was calm: "Go outside and look for your brother's finger."

Nauseated, crying so hard she could barely see, Adrienne searched the grass, praying she wouldn't miss it.

Then the phone rang again: they'd found the missing finger on the floor of the car. Relief washed over her, but the image of blood in the yard never left.

Barry Jr. was medevaced to a hospital in North Jersey. Surgeons reattached the ring and middle finger with rods.

To this day, he can't bend the tips, and his middle finger is shorter than it should be. On a man 6'5" with size 15 feet, those stubby fingers are a sight. He still points with them constantly, just to torment his siblings, until they swat his hand away and laugh.

After that, Sandra never made him cut the grass again. The rest of them picked up the duty. She was an equal opportunist, yes; but she wasn't cruel.

The house was joy and chaos. Parties and fights. Chores and accidents. Neighbors and cops. Grit and laughter.

Belonging meant you worked, you fought, you celebrated, and you endured together.

Just like Felipe, everyone who belonged there learned the same thing: you could roam, but you came home.

Sandra made it possible. She let the nights run long, but always on her terms; flashing the lights when it was time to shut it down, stepping in when things got wild, reminding everyone whose house it was.

The block loved her because she loved them first. Their home was more than walls and furniture. It was safety.

It was fun. It was proof that joy could live even after a crash.

## CHAPTER 24
# AIN'T NO HOOD LIKE MOTHERHOOD

Sandra was what Adrienne would call a basic Christian. She believed in God but was more spiritual than religious.

Growing up, they were more than Seasonal Saints, who typically only attend church on holidays, but Sandra was far from a Holy Roller.

Church was a Sunday morning babysitter when Sandra needed a break. In Germany, she would put Adrienne and Barry Jr. on the church bus that came on base to pick up kids for Sunday school.

Sandra never joined them and never showed up later for the main service.

As teenagers, it felt more like payback. If they stayed out late on Saturday night, she would make them get up for church on Sunday morning, yelling, "If you can party all night, you can get up and go to church in the morning."

Even though Calvary Baptist Church was less than a mile away, they were always late.

The kids never sat next to her because she always fell

asleep during the service. If the pastor prayed too long or there were too many testimonies, they could hear her snoring in the pew.

Sometimes Adrienne would sit behind her and tap her shoulder, which startled Sandra awake and made her fuss, "Stop tapping me, I'm awake!"

Sandra never made them read the Bible, and Adrienne isn't sure she ever saw her mother open it except to follow along in church.

A huge gold Bible sat on the schrank, open to a random chapter and verse with a red ribbon marking the spot. When Adrienne dusted, she would turn the pages so the book wouldn't stick together.

The main way she praised God was through music.

Sandra always had music in the house.

That was something she and Barry shared. They owned top-of-the-line audio systems, speakers, and stacks of records. There were tape decks and a reel-to-reel; a device that records and plays back sound using magnetic tape spooled between two reels.

On any given Sunday morning, gospel music played throughout the house, often serving as the alarm to get the kids up and moving.

Sometimes the music sent a message, depending on Sandra's mood.

When she played Shirley Caesar's *No Charge*, she let the whole house hear it.

The song told the story of a mother listing everything she had poured into her child, only to explain that none of it carried a price because love itself was the payment.

Everyone understood why Sandra loved that song so deeply. Her sacrifices came with no bill and no expectation of repayment.

It wasn't until the kids were grown and gone that she began attending church regularly, sometimes taking the boarders who still lived in the house.

She even joined the finance ministry, which was ironic, since managing money had never been her strength.

Even with all that, she prayed and welcomed prayer from others.

So, when Sandra stepped into motherhood's hardest season she believed she was covered by the prayers of her sister Pat.

Pat went to God on her behalf, asking for strength to endure the breaking of her marriage and the weight of raising four children alone.

That prayer became Sandra's armor. It steadied her when the house was too quiet at night and when the days stretched long under the pressure of holding everything together.

Sandra poured all her energy into raising her children, but raising four children alone came with challenges.

# ADRIENNE

Adrienne carried the divorce like a weapon, using it as license to act out.

Sandra, worn down by the constant rebellion, once told her, "If I could do it all over again, I wouldn't have any girls."

As the only daughter, those words stuck with Adrienne like glue.

She knew she had been awful, rebellious, and difficult for no real reason except anger. She was mad at how things had gone down, mad that no one ever discussed it, mad that everyone pretended life was fine when it wasn't.

She was just mad.

Her rebellion showed in little ways that stacked up.

She would sneak out. She would lie about where she was going and ask her best friend Kimmy to cover for her.

She thought she was grown and underestimated Sandra at every turn.

What Adrienne forgot was that Sandra had been a teenage girl once too. She also forgot that Mary said Sandra was the only one of her six children who never got in trouble, not from perfection but from learning early to obey, stay quiet, and cover her tracks.

Adrienne never stood a chance.

One night, Adrienne decided to sneak out to see a boy she was messing with in Red Bank, riding her brother's bike under the cover of darkness. Down in the boy's basement, they were fooling around when his mother came to the top of the steps calling down, asking if he was there and what he was doing. He brushed her off, saying he was just looking for something.

What neither of them knew was that Sandra had already called the mother. She had discovered Adrienne was gone and knowing her daughter better than Adrienne knew herself, anticipated exactly where she went.

Adrienne pedaled back home, slipped inside, and felt proud that she had managed to outslick her mother.

But Sandra always played the long game.

The next morning, she came into Adrienne's room and told her to get dressed because they were going to breakfast. Adrienne assumed they were headed to a diner. Instead, her stomach dropped when they pulled up to the boy's house.

The boy's mother opened the door with a grin that told Adrienne they were caught. She and Sandra welcomed Adrienne inside and, standing in front of both teenagers, declared, "Good morning. We're making you lovers breakfast. Feel free to go into the bedroom and take care of your business while we finish cooking."

Mortified, Adrienne and the boy went into the room and sat side by side in silence while the mothers laughed in the kitchen, frying eggs, bacon, sausage, and toast. Eventually, they knocked on the door with a polite, cutting question; "Are you finished with your business? Breakfast was ready."

The four of them sat at the table, the smell of food heavy in the air, the silence thicker than the grits on the plates. That meal marked the end of that teenage romance and a lesson she never forgot.

Adrienne continued to test Sandra throughout her teenage years, but the victory was always Sandra's.

The last real challenge came when Adrienne was eighteen, and a freshman at Montclair State. Convinced she was grown; she slipped back into town one weekend to spend the night with her boyfriend at a local hotel.

She assumed no one would know, but Sandra had eyes everywhere.

Someone who knew Sandra spotted Adrienne and the boyfriend and passed the word along.

The next morning, Adrienne, in her boldness, decided to stop by the house, pretending she was homesick and just wanted to say hi.

Sandra confronted Adrienne, asking her directly what her plan was.

"What do you want to do with your life?"

Adrienne, standing in the arrogance of her youth, answered, "I'm quitting school. I'm going to get an apartment and live with my boyfriend."

Sandra didn't argue. She simply told Adrienne she had something for her and to wait in her room.

A few minutes later, Sandra knocked on the door, leather belt in hand, and gave Adrienne the worst whipping she had ever received.

It wasn't her usual measured punishment.

When it was over, Sandra looked her in the eye and said, "You're grown now. You can make your own decisions. If you want to go live with some little nigga in an apartment, go right ahead."

In Sandra's expected style, she hugged her, said "Mommy loves you," and walked out of the room.

That declaration shook Adrienne more than the belt. The finality in Sandra's voice made the stakes clear.

Adrienne jumped into her little brown Datsun and drove straight back to Montclair State. She never looked back.

From that moment forward, she was determined to stay in school and finish what she started. She went on to earn not only her bachelor's degree but three master's degrees.

Sandra's victory was not in breaking her daughter's spirit but in setting her on a path she could not turn from.

In the end, Adrienne finally understood what her mother had been saying all along, "You can't outslick a slickster."

## SONNY

From the start, Sonny's place in Sandra's house was different.

When Franny died, grief followed him out, but Sandra pulled him close, claimed him, and gave him the one thing he had never known: stability. He wasn't hers by birth, he was hers by choice.

That choice cut deeper the day Barry gathered the children to say he was leaving. His heavy voice filled the room, and when he turned to Sonny, and said "Come with me," it sounded like a summons. But Sonny refused.

He stayed.

His bond with Sandra was sealed in that defiance, a love not born of blood but of loyalty.

The streets tugged at him.

He tried hustling small-time out of Sandra's house, until the day he dropped a clip of vials, small bottles of drugs linked together in a row.

Sandra summoned him to her office, the glass in her hand, her voice sharp as stone.

"What is this?"

"It's a friend's," Sonny lied.

Sandra wasn't fooled. "You're not getting it back."

When more vials appeared, her patience ended. "You're my son, and I love you. But you cannot have this in my house. You have to go."

Sonny left without a fight, knowing she was right. He drifted and got arrested. Sandra made her position clear.

"I will visit you once while you're in jail. One time. Then I will pick you up when your sentence is done."

Adrienne even wrote him a letter during his sentence, firm and unyielding: if he planned to return to the streets, he was not to come back to the house. Alongside the letter, she sent him the book Black Men: Obsolete, Single, Dangerous? A message as clear as her words.

Sandra kept her word.

She came once, bringing pictures, money, and a letter, then disappeared until the day she parked down the street from the jail gates. Eighteen months behind bars, followed by five years of probation, became the weight he carried into a new life.

Sonny walked to her car, climbed in, and heard the words that mattered: "Welcome home. I want you to get yourself together. Don't worry about anything else. You'll be taken care of but get yourself together."

That moment marked a turn.

Sonny decided to pursue culinary school, and Sandra backed him fully. She drove him to Maryland herself, made sure he had what he needed, and reminded him, sometimes teasing and sometimes dead serious, that support came with responsibility.

Sandra kept him steady through it, making sure he showed up where he was supposed to and reminding him not to waste the second chance.

Sonny never forgot any of it.

He shared his jail story without shame, quick to remind people that the tie and shirt he wore later in life did not erase where he had been.

What defined him most was not the time he served but the mother who drew hard lines and then lifted him back up when he was ready to stand.

# BARRY JR.

Barry Jr. was her emotional child.

Like Adrienne, he carried the weight of their father's absence, but at ten years old, emotions showed up as actions, not words. He was a big kid with a quick temper, prone to tantrums that left holes in walls or broken objects in his wake.

Sandra understood his pain, but she never excused the behavior. She shut it down fast.

One morning Adrienne spotted a note taped to the refrigerator: "I'm leaving, no one loves me in this house!"

Barry Jr. had packed his red bag labeled "Lil Dude," stuffed with pennies, and decided he was running away.

Adrienne told her mother, and the search began.

Sandra hit the streets in the car while Adrienne searched on foot, calling out his name so he would know they were looking.

Adrienne crossed the Field toward Cherry Street, only to be met by a pack of dogs. They cornered her, barking and snapping, until she scrambled onto the roof of an abandoned car. She saw Sandra's car turning down the street and flagged her down. Sandra jumped out, chased off the dogs, and pulled Adrienne into the car so they could continue searching together.

Hours passed with no sign of Barry Jr.

Back home, Sandra prepared to call the police. Before she could dial, the phone rang. It was her neighbor and friend, Mrs. Catley. Barry Jr. hadn't gone far at all; he was hiding in their backyard across the street.

All that panic, hours of searching, and Adrienne barely escaping a dog attack, only to find out Barry Jr.'s grand runaway plan ended in the neighbor's yard.

His teenage years only brought more turmoil.

When Barry Jr. was in eleventh grade, a pep rally sparked his next lesson learned.

The school was already divided, with skinheads, white students known for shaved heads, boots, and open racism, on one side, and Five Percenters, Black students rooted in pride, discipline, and the teachings of the Nation of Gods and Earths, on the other. All it took was one punch to ignite the fuse.

The pep rally ended with one of the skinheads getting jumped.

By the next day, Barry's crew was ready. When the skinheads sent a messenger through the halls saying, "If any of you niggers want to fight, come outside," there was no turning back.

The parking lot became a standoff.

On one side, the skinheads lined up along the track bus. On the other, Barry Jr. and his crew squared their shoulders, fists ready.

Silence hung for a beat, the kind that makes your stomach tighten.

Then his boy stepped forward, swung a trapper keeper, and cracked a hulking white boy, square in the face.

Chaos erupted. Bodies collided, fists slammed, glass shattered.

Barry Jr. remembered grabbing one boy, hurling him through a window, then turning to drop another in the hallway as the brawl found its way back into the school.

The fight spilled into every corner, through the halls, across the floors, out the exits. They ran out of the school and through the neighborhood, sneakers pounding the pavement, hearts racing, knuckles split, adrenaline still buzzing.

They thought they got away.

The next day, two paddy wagons sat parked outside the school.

Officers went room to room calling names.

Barry Jr. and the rest were marched out.

Sandra came to the police station to get her son.

She wasn't smiling. She wasn't soft.

"I'm not fighting for you because you were right," she told him, her voice even.

"I'm fighting for you because they don't see you, Barry. They see your skin, and they will bury you for it if you let them. Don't hand them the shovel."

At home, she pressed harder.

"That anger you've got; it will strip every blessing out of your life. You hear me? Every single one."

Barry Jr.'s coach echoed Sandra's warning.

"Barry, you're standing at a line. Cross it wrong, and it's prison. Stay right, and you've got a chance."

Barry Jr. had always been the physical one; breaking bones, busting knuckles, too quick to fight.

Seeing his mother weary, carrying his trouble on her shoulders, started to sink in.

Basketball gave him an outlet, but her voice was louder than the roar of the streets.

By his twenties, the wild temper was gone.

He spoke softer now.

He avoided anger and tried not to raise his voice.

Sandra's words stayed etched in his mind: anger destroys, restraint preserves. That restraint became the measure of the man.

## CARLOS

If Barry Jr. was shaped by rage, Carlos was shaped by Sandra's steady hand.

He was her baby boy, born so young into the unraveling of his parents' marriage that he had no memory of ever living with his father.

Unlike his older siblings, Carlos grew up rooted on the Avenue from the start, same street, same school, same friends.

He was spoiled in a way, protected by his older brothers and sister.

But Sandra never let protection turn into passivity.

Baby boy or not, Carlos was hers to raise.

She wouldn't push the responsibility on her older children.

"He's my son, not yours," she would say.

"I'll get a sitter, or I won't go. You're not raising him. I am."

Still, Carlos tested her.

One afternoon, after doing something that earned him a spanking, Sandra sent him to his room.

Instead of obeying, Carlos bolted out the front door. Standing on the lawn, shouting for help.

"Somebody call Child Protective Services!"

Sandra stepped calmly onto the porch, arms folded, her voice even.

"You better hope they do call CPS and take you away. Because if they don't, you're going to regret it."

The words froze him. He wasn't prepared for her to mean it.

Quietly, Carlos turned back toward the house and went to his room to wait for his punishment.

As a college student at North Carolina Central University, a Historically Black institution founded in 1910 and known for its academic excellence, research, and commitment to liberal arts education for African Americans, Carlos further tested his boundaries.

Instead of showing up for class, he decided to chase the fantasy of being a dorm-room kingpin.

The hustle was short-lived.

The Dean of Students caught wind of what was happening and quickly involved the Durham police. It wasn't going to be tolerated, not on his campus, not in his dorms.

One evening, Sandra got the call every parent dreads.

Carlos admitted he was being kicked out. No excuses, no way around it.

Sandra wasted no time. She grabbed her keys, jumped in the car, and drove south through the night.

On the way she picked up Adrienne, who was living in Maryland, and the two of them pushed on until they reached Durham.

What they found was more than disappointing. It was shocking.

Carlos stood there looking like a caricature ripped from a cheap drug movie; head full of braids, clothes sagging, and an attitude to match.

Sandra was not impressed.

Sandra immediately requested a meeting with the Dean.

The man did not mince words.

Either she took Carlos home that night, or he would be turned over to the police.

Then came the part that stuck hard.

The Dean told Carlos he was banned from the entire state of North Carolina. If he ever set foot there again and was caught, he would go straight to jail.

It echoed the ultimatum his father, Barry once faced from the judge many years earlier. His father wasn't much older than he was when he faced that judge, but the difference was clear. The Dean cared about the future of Black boys, and the judge did not.

Sandra left the office fuming, not just about the so-called drug dealing but about the wasted opportunity. She had sacrificed too much, fought too hard, for her children to squander their futures.

On the long drive north, she let Carlos have it.

She cursed him out until her throat hurt, then laid down the law; those braids better be out of his head before they crossed the Delaware Memorial Bridge, or he would wish she had left him in a Durham jail cell.

By the time they reached Maryland, Sandra posed the question she had already asked three of her children before him; "What are your plans? Because you cannot stay here and do nothing."

Carlos knew she meant it.

Faced with her ultimatum, he pivoted.

He enrolled in a local school, shifted his focus, and chose to study Information Technology and Networking.

It wasn't the path she had hoped he would take when she first dropped him off at college, but it was a step toward redemption and proof that, even after failure, Sandra was determined to push her children back toward possibility.

That was the balance of being Sandra's baby, love without indulgence, discipline without apology.

Spoiled or not, Carlos and Sandra were yin and yang; inseparable, interdependent, and constantly interacting to create a dynamic balance.

He was the one who would leave home but never drift far, the son who circled close and always came back. In time, Carlos would be more than her baby boy.

He would be Sandra's hero.

# SANDRA

Sandra's journey through that season of motherhood was a gauntlet; four children, four different battles, and one unshakable resolve.

Adrienne tested her wit, Sonny tested her limits, Barry Jr. tested her patience, and Carlos tested her endurance. Each child carried the weight of a broken marriage in their own way, and each one tried her strength.

Motherhood was its own kind of Brick City, tough but unbreakable, and Sandra held it together with the armor her sister Pat's prayers placed on her. Faith, discipline, and a fierce love that refused to quit.

Every rule, every punishment, every sacrifice was her way of keeping them alive long enough to grow into the people they were destined to be.

Growing up in Newark, New Jersey, was a tough hood, but Sandra learned what mothers already know.

To be a mother, you must be tougher, louder, and more loyal than any gangster, because at the end of the day, ain't no hood like motherhood.

# CHAPTER 25
# A THIN LINE BETWEEN LOVE & HATE

It would be many years later, with a new heart and a third wife, that Barry finally saw the error of his ways.

His new wife held up the mirror he had long avoided, pointing out the dysfunction, the patterns, the psychosis that had shaped his life. She urged him to make amends and take at least one step toward the past he had abandoned.

At her insistence, Barry picked up the phone and called Sandra.

What he said exactly was between the two of them. But imagine it went this way.

His hands trembled, the same way they had the night he took her to a restaurant to confess, nervously weighing every word, afraid of her answer.

"Sandra... it's Barry."

A long pause. In that silence, Barry felt every mile of distance between who they had been and who they had become.

"I know I don't deserve your time. I know I don't deserve your forgiveness. But I need to say this."

His voice cracked, stripped of performance.

"I was wrong. I broke what we had. I hurt you; I hurt the kids, I hurt myself. And for years I told myself it was someone else's fault. It wasn't. It was mine."

He took a breath, then said what had weighed longest.

"You deserved a husband who honored you. The children deserved a father who showed up. You gave me everything, and I threw it away. I can't undo it, Sandra, but I need you to know I am sorry. From the bottom of the new heart I was given, I apologize."

Sandra listened without interruption.

She had forgiven him long before, not because she forgot, but because she knew he was lost.

She understood years ago that he was no longer the high school sweetheart she once loved.

She also knew bitterness would poison her if she let it stay.

Forgiveness, for her, was survival. It was a way to model for her children what she wanted them to learn. If she didn't forgive, if she didn't show love even when it wasn't deserved, how would they?

Her reply was quiet but steady, echoing the grace she had shown him in that restaurant years earlier.

"Barry, I forgave you a long time ago."

With that, a burden lifted. The bitterness between them thinned. For a moment, they understood each other again.

It was the only true apology he would ever give.

He never had a reckoning with his mother before her death.

With his sisters, the silence was even heavier.

Janice had done what he would not. She took Crystal without question, raised her, fought for her, and loved her. For that, Barry owed his sister a debt he never paid, a truth left unspoken, carried like another ghost in the ruins of his choices.

Dina carried her own scars. First as a child, when Barry's spanking crossed the line into violence, and later as an adult, when he smacked her across the face in a fit of rage. He never tried to repair either wound.

He had no words for Laney.

She hated him for being the One Son, resented the place he held, and made sure he felt it in every exchange. Her words were sharp, venomous, and no apology would have mattered. Nothing he could have said would have pierced that wall of anger or contempt she had for him.

Franny was the only sister he tried to do right by. Even though he failed her by leaving her son, he knew she would be satisfied knowing Sonny was well cared for by Sandra.

In the end, Barry's life with Halle was a house of cards, built in secrecy, balanced on lies, and doomed from the start. Each choice pulled another card from the fragile frame until nothing remained but collapse.

What he mistook for freedom was ruin. What he thought he gained turned to dust. The curse of that union did not end with its fall; it scattered through the lives of his children, each of them left to sift through the wreckage he left behind.

Yet for all that collapse, his call to Sandra remained. It was not redemption, but it was release. The words he offered her became the line that separated his chaos from her strength, his ruin from her rebuilding.

Sandra carried no illusions.

She raised her children, built her life without him, and told the truth by the way she lived. Yet in hearing his apology, she allowed herself one final grace; to let him go without hatred.

So, it ended where it began, with Sandra holding steady and Barry speaking the words she was owed all along.

It is a burden Barry will always bear, a weight that

stretches beyond his lifetime, carried in the protection of his mother, the silence of his sisters, the strength of his children, the shadow of Halle, and the grace of Sandra, woven through every generation that shares the bloodline of his love, his lies, and his legacy.

## CHAPTER 26
# JERSEY STRONG

Loss is an interesting thing when it touches someone you care about, someone you love, someone who loved you back. There's pain, but it's clean; it comes with memory and meaning. You grieve what was shared.

But loss feels different when love was uncertain, when affection came in fragments or not at all.

It becomes tangled, part sorrow, part relief, part confusion. You mourn the idea of what could have been rather than what was.

That kind of loss doesn't move through you; it lingers, settling in the spaces where love should have lived.

On Monday, October 22, 2012, a storm began to form deep in the western Caribbean. What started as a tropical wave gathered speed and force, feeding on warm waters and shifting the winds.

By nightfall, it had a name: Sandy.

As it moved north toward Jamaica, it strengthened, a growing mass of pressure and power. Although no one knew how far it would reach, the weight of it could already be felt, a storm that seemed to announce itself before ever touching land.

The call came early, cutting through the quiet of a Monday morning.

Her mother's mother, Mary was gone.

Adrienne always felt like she only had one grandmother and now she had none.

The night before, Adrienne thought about calling but decided to wait.

It was Uncle Porgie's birthday, and she wanted to give him his moment.

Nanna's birthday was only two days away, and she planned to be one of the many voices filling the day with laughter and love.

Interestingly enough, Uncle Porgie was the only one of the six Scott children to sustain a long marriage.

He and Aunt Earline had been married for more than fifty years.

Adrienne admired their longevity. It made her own twenty-one-year marriage feel less like a final achievement and more like ongoing training.

But by sunrise, celebration had turned to sorrow.

The news left her motionless.

Grief arrived without warning, heavy and absolute. She leaned into her husband's chest until his shirt was drenched with her tears.

Mary was the family's center. Everybody's favorite. Every grandchild claimed her as their Nanna.

Wherever she was, became home.

Thanksgiving, Christmas, Easter, birthdays, and graduations all stitched the family together in those moments.

Mary's house was a gathering place, always warm, always ready.

# THE ONE SON

Pots clattered, laughter echoed, and voices so loud you could hear them from the street.

The kids could be as loud as they wanted at Nanna's house, because if they didn't yell over their cousins, they wouldn't be heard.

She cooked like company was coming even when no one was expected. Her table and her heart were never empty.

Her death shattered the flow of their lives. It was sudden. It was swift. It was unexpected.

There had been fainting spells, but this one ended differently. She fainted in the bathroom and hit her head when she fell.

On October 24, which would have been Mary's 82nd birthday, the storm grew into a hurricane and made landfall near Kingston, Jamaica. It crossed back into open water, gaining force, swelling into a Category 2 storm before striking Cuba at Category 3 strength.

What should have been a day of celebration became a day of fury, as wind and water rose in unison. It felt almost symbolic, as if the heavens themselves were shifting to make room for her.

Adrienne moved through those days like someone floating just above the ground, present but unreachable. The world kept turning, but she stood still inside it, her sorrow suspended in slow motion, like a scene out of a Spike Lee Joint, where the character glides through chaos, untouched yet completely undone.

Then on Friday, October 26, another call came.

Her father's mother, Dorothy was gone.

When news of Dorothy's passing came, Adrienne felt no shock, no tears, only stillness.

The grief was complicated, tangled in years of silence and disappointment. There was no peace to gather, no warmth to remember. Her death marked the end of a chapter that had never been written with love.

The next day, Sandy wavered, briefly losing power before regaining strength as it pushed toward the U.S. coast.

Then came the turn, the sharp westward curve meteorologists called the "left hook."

In the early hours of October 29, Sandy came ashore near Brigantine, New Jersey, just northeast of Atlantic City, carrying hurricane-force winds and the weight of an entire ocean behind it.

It felt biblical, as if heaven and ocean were in conversation, rising and roaring in agreement. The sky mourned, the sea answered, everything about the family changed and seemed to be carried away in the swell.

The storm drifted inland for days, weakening slowly until November 2, when it was finally absorbed by another system.

By then the damage was done.

Two mothers gone in the same week. The symmetry was haunting.

Barry and Sandra were connected again, bound by something neither of them could control.

This time it wasn't blood or marriage that tied them, but loss.

Both of their mothers leaving this earth within days of each other felt almost deliberate in its timing, as if the universe had drawn a final line between them, two lives still intertwined, even in farewell.

The difference between them was clear even in their funerals.

Mary's service was held the last week of October, just as the air began to turn cold.

It was beautiful, one of love, reflection, and remembrance.

It carried a spirit of gratitude that Mary had chosen them to be her family.

The sanctuary was filled with warmth and light, overflowing with love, music and memories. Every song, every word, every tear felt like worship. The air carried peace, not pain. It was the kind of home going that reminded everyone what a life well-lived looked like.

In contrast, Dorothy was always cold toward Adrienne, a chill that never thawed. There was no warmth in her hugs, no softness in her words. The distance between them wasn't born of time; it was born of choice.

Adrienne never forgave her for her part in the conspiracy that helped to destroy their family, for using Janice as part of the deception, and for always covering for her father.

Dorothy's loyalty to Barry had come at everyone else's expense, and Sandra paid the highest price.

Sometime earlier, Adrienne reached out to Dorothy.

Her voice on the phone had been polite but hollow, like a door cracked open just enough to prove it could still move.

When Adrienne mentioned visiting, silence filled the line. Then came the faint sound of Janice whispering in the background. That told her everything she needed to know.

Then Dorothy's final words, measured, careful, unmistakable; "I don't want you to visit me."

It landed like a verdict. Even at the end, Dorothy refused her.

Adrienne believed Janice dictated the moment, but Dorothy allowed it.

Rejection was still rejection.

Adrienne hung up and sat in silence, staring at the phone as if waiting for it to ring again. It didn't.

The rejection wasn't loud; it was quiet and sharp, the kind that cuts without sound. She felt the same ache she'd carried since childhood, the same confusion that came from loving people who refused to love her back.

That call confirmed what she had always known. Dorothy's heart was closed to her, and not even an olive branch would open it.

On that day, Adrienne decided the next time she saw Dorothy would be in a casket, and even then, only if her father asked.

Adrienne stopped expecting anything from her. The hope of reconciliation faded into acceptance, the quiet kind that comes when you finally understand who people are and who they will never be.

She realized that Dorothy's distance shaped her as much as Sandra's strength had. One taught her how to hold on. The other taught her when to let go.

Dorothy's funeral felt more like a courtesy than a farewell, marked by formality, restraint and unspoken tension. The air was heavy, not with sorrow, but with all the words that had gone unsaid. Adrienne stood quietly, not out of mourning, but out of respect for the lineage that had brought her here, even in its brokenness.

Dorothy's funeral took place early at Peaceful Zion Baptist Church in East Orange, New Jersey.

For Adrienne, the name Peaceful Zion felt like a lie everyone agreed to tell. There had never been peace in Dorothy's house, only secrets and silence dressed up as order.

Even in death, the setting felt misplaced.

The service belonged to no one and everyone, a generic farewell for a woman who had spent her life keeping people at a distance.

Adrienne doubted Dorothy had ever been a member there. It was fitting in its own way; impersonal, detached, and quiet.

# THE ONE SON

The funeral unfolded like a scene from a reality show, scripted chaos packaged as sincerity.

Janice ran the program like a producer on set, ready to perform at any moment. Barry, the One Son, stood apart. His name appeared once in the printed program, small and buried in the middle.

No pastor presided.

Janice claimed the pulpit, high above the congregation, reading the obituary, offering the eulogy, and calling people up at random.

What followed was not a service but a spectacle, part confession, part open mic, part therapy session.

Barry wasn't asked to speak or maybe he wasn't allowed.

The One Son, her reflection, her contradiction, was silenced. It felt deliberate, like a final punishment for the sins of being chosen and being flawed.

At the repast, the performance continued. A PowerPoint slideshow ran on a loop, filled with photos of Dorothy's life.

None included Barry.

The cemetery was soaked and unsteady, the ground still waterlogged from Sandy's surge.

When the casket was lowered, the earth filled it with water and mud.

There was no vault, the concrete or metal container used to protect a casket from the weight of the earth. Without it, the soil pressed in, the ground unsettled, and the cold wind carried the weight of what could not be contained.

The scene carried a grim poetry.

The grave itself mirrored Dorothy's life; restless and unresolved, full of turbulence. The same water that had flooded the Shore now filled her final resting place, as if the storm had followed her, unwilling to let her leave untouched.

It felt like judgment and reflection at once, a reckoning for all that had been stirred, a baptism for all that was never made clean.

For Adrienne, the contrast between Mary and Dorothy was unrelenting.

One had built warmth; the other had built walls.

One left comfort; the other left confusion.

But that was her truth.

Her cousins told another story.

On Facebook, their words painted Dorothy as gentle and loving. They called her Queen. They used hearts and halos. To them, she was a legacy.

To Adrienne, she was a lesson.

It confirmed what she had always known that Dorothy's resentment had a single direction.

It wasn't the family she despised; it was Adrienne.

The firstborn of the One Son. The Dark One.

The child who once stood between Dorothy and her only son was now grown, and Dorothy's time had come to an end.

The battle she orchestrated was finally over.

With her gone, Barry's only real link to his sisters vanished too.

Whatever came next would depend on them.

In the days that followed, New Jersey was unrecognizable.

The same week the family lost their mothers, the storm that bore Sandra's name tore through the coast they called home.

Streets flooded, power vanished, and memories washed away with the tide.

Neighbors who lost everything helped one another dig out from the wreckage. The Red Cross and local churches set up shelters and food stations.

Then came the rebuilding, homes lifted, shorelines reinforced, maps redrawn to mark the damage.

# THE ONE SON

What had been grief in one family became grief across a state.

Just as Barry and Sandra faced what was gone, so did New Jersey.

All were left to rebuild from what the storm had taken. But Jersey has always been strong.

Even in ruin, people showed up for each other, patching walls, sharing generators, cooking meals on sidewalks. The spirit that had carried them through every hard season rose again, proving what everyone from the Shore Points to Paramus along the Garden State Parkway already knew; Jersey may bend, but it does not break.

So many drives from Montclair State, off Normal Avenue, heading toward the Shore Points on the Parkway nearly fifty miles away.

So many late nights, driving down the Parkway in that little brown Datsun, window cracked just enough to stay awake, Black Sheep's *The Choice Is Yours* blasting loud enough to rattle the doors.

The beat didn't just thump, it insisted. It kept her alert, kept her moving, kept sleep from winning. The kind of music that made her feel wide awake and alive, like the night itself was pushing her to stay present long enough to make it home.

Now the same road carried only reflection. The state had changed. So had she.

Her family, like her state, had weathered its storms, some born of nature and others born of blood. Both bore scars, but both endured.

On this drive, she chose Dianne Reeves' *Better Days*.

The song wrapped around her like memory, pulling her back to the Avenue in the Fruit Bowl where life once felt safe and sure.

She could see her grandmother Mary leaning over the

stove, cooking eggs with the precision of someone who understood that love lived in the details.

Every stir was a lesson in care. Every sprinkle was a reminder that patience was part of the recipe.

As the chorus rose, the message hit her the way it always did.

The song was a push toward hope, a gentle nudge toward holding on a little longer. Adrienne felt it settle into her bones. It was her Nanna speaking through the music, reminding her that endurance was their inheritance. Better days were still possible if she kept pressing forward, even when the road went dark.

Somewhere on that long stretch headed south on the Parkway, Adrienne heard the whisper of Mary's voice, steady and sure.

"The Lord is still in control, baby."

She whispered back, "I know, Nanna. I know."

It started as a slogan but became a promise.

Strength here wasn't loud or pretty; it was survival.

It was rebuilding in the dark, holding family together through loss, standing in the wreckage, and daring to believe that what came next could still be possible.

The phrase that would later cover billboards and car bumpers after the storm lived within her, Jersey Strong.

Being Jersey Strong was never about what was lost. It was about what remained: faith, family, and the will to keep driving forward because the road always leads home.

## CHAPTER 27
# A SONG FOR MOMMA

Now Sandra's four children were grown. The house no longer echoed with slammed doors, school alarms, or her voice calling from the bottom of the stairs.

These days, Adrienne often sits in quiet reflection, listening to the stillness that replaced all that noise, wondering how a home once so full could feel both peaceful and impossibly vast.

In 2002, seventeen years after the divorce, the same length of time that Sandra and Barry had been married, Adrienne felt the symmetry settle over her like a quiet truth.

The family sat outside in the waiting room while Adrienne sat in pre-op, reflecting on how the story seemed to circle back on itself.

The first seventeen years had built a family. The next seventeen had taught them how to stand on their own, how to find their voices separate from Barry.

She thought about how life repeats its lessons. Years earlier, Barry had been the one in a hospital bed waiting for a new heart, a moment that shifted his course and softened his view of the world.

Now it was Sandra whose body was failing, her kidneys weakening, and Adrienne realized this was the moment when the strength of everything her mother had built, every sacrifice, every lesson, every ounce of resilience, would reveal its true depth.

Sandra lived at a pace that left no room for sickness.

Diabetes followed her for years, but after pneumonia her numbers changed. Her vision blurred at night, and the lights along Route 35 turned into halos. She was always thirsty. Then she started falling asleep behind the wheel. She joked about it, but her body was already warning her.

The doctor said dialysis. Three days a week, four hours each session. Machines hummed while the family kept watch.

"You don't feel pain," she told them.

"You just lie there and the machine does what your body can't."

Her blood pressure refused to come down. Then came the words that rearrange a family.

"You need a transplant."

Everyone volunteered. Her children, nieces, nephews, even friends from Calvary Baptist Church.

Sandra shook her head.

"I'm not the kind of person who looks for a favor." But she didn't have to ask.

Adrienne was the match.

Adrienne said yes without hesitation.

"If you want a kidney, you've got one."

The call came on the morning of a friend's funeral. Sandra took the timing as divine.

"God took one life and gave one back," she said.

She gathered everyone before they left for the service.

"I have a perfect match." When she told them it was Adrienne, the room filled with tears and prayer.

On July 10, 2002, Sandra and Adrienne were admitted to St. Barnabas Medical Center in Livingston, a national leader in kidney and pancreas transplantation.

That day, mother and daughter became bound by more than blood.

Adrienne went first. Hugs, prayer, the soft sound of gurney wheels.

Then Sandra.

Six hours later, two bodies shared one story.

That night they walked the hospital corridor together, IV poles moving beside them.

They would both recover at Mary's house, the best place for love and healing.

Within weeks Adrienne was back home in Maryland.

Sandra returned to work, walking two miles a day and checking her sugar every morning.

"The kidney fits like it has always been there," she said. "All glory to God."

Beneath that private miracle was a larger truth.

Black patients made up more than a third of the national kidney waitlist but received only about a fifth of the transplants. Over ninety percent of people on dialysis were African American. The need was higher, the wait longer, the odds lower.

Diabetes and hypertension struck harder.

Success rates rose when Black recipients received kidneys from Black donors, yet most donors were white. Many Black patients didn't know they could register while on dialysis. Some thought they were already on the list when the process hadn't even begun.

Physicians sometimes delayed the discussion altogether. Fear, mistrust, and history filled the gaps.

Sandra and Adrienne did not argue with statistics. They changed them.

The kidney held, and so did Sandra's faith.

For twelve years she lived in gratitude, proof that prayer and perseverance could outlast prediction until the next test of faith arrived.

The call came from Carlos. It was 2014.

Sandra had gotten lost driving through the neighborhood she had known since the 80s. A childhood friend found her parked, praying out loud for directions home.

At the house she began repeating herself, forgetting meals, losing time.

Scans confirmed a tumor.

A lymphoma formed in the center of Sandra's brain, a side effect of the anti-rejection medication that protected the kidney.

Surgery wasn't an option. Chemotherapy and radiation followed.

The bold, independent woman who had run her house and everyone else's became a dependent patient. Her body and mind aged decades in months.

Doctors gave her one year to live.

She told them, "Those doctors don't know anything. God decides when I leave this earth."

She refused to say the word "cancer." When asked, she would shrug.

"That's what they say," she'd reply with an attitude.

She lived another ten years.

To let Sandra tell it, she was still a Bad Mama Jama; still unforgettable in every room she entered.

She was still sexy and sharp, funny and fearless, a woman

who carried her own rhythm and brought the party with her wherever she went.

Carlos became her hero.

He lived with her, cared for her, and learned everything she needed.

He became a certified nursing assistant and immersed himself in her daily care. He watched her closely, anticipating her needs before she spoke them. His patience was steady, his presence constant.

Sonny moved his family from Maryland back to New Jersey so he could be near her.

Sandra had supported his dream of becoming a chef, and now he used those skills to make sure her nutritional needs were met. He filled her kitchen with the smell of home, soups, stews, and comfort that nourished the body and spirit alike.

Barry Jr. came from Connecticut to do the heavy lifting, fixing what broke, keeping the house in order, and helping with errands and repairs.

Adrienne handled the logistics and paperwork, managing the appointments, medications, insurance calls, and endless forms that came with care.

Sandra raised them to be a team. She never realized the team she built would one day be for her.

Her faith guided them all. She showed them how to fight without bitterness and to accept help without shame.

She believed healing came in many forms, that love itself was medicine.

Each prayer, each act of care, each shared meal became part of that healing.

The doctors called her case extraordinary. Her children called it faith.

She'd say, "I told you so!"

Sandra's days were filled with laughter, prayer, and

moments of quiet joy. She never allowed sickness to define her or dictate the atmosphere of her home.

When her hands trembled, she lifted them anyway.

When her voice faltered, she whispered.

Even in the hardest times, she would look around and say, "We are blessed."

Her children believed her.

Decline came in fragments.

Adrienne and her brothers never wavered.

They learned how to care for a woman who had never taken direction from anyone.

She was still in charge, and no matter how she felt, she made sure they remembered she was the mother and they were her children.

Don't get it twisted.

Sandra often visited Adrienne in her dreams.

Sometimes it began with that childhood voice calling up the stairs; "Queen Elizabeth! Wake up!"

The tone changed with the reason; gentle for breakfast, sharp for yard work, aggravated if she had to call her more than one time.

Those calls had shaped Adrienne's childhood, and now they followed her into sleep.

In another dream, she was on a work trip, and the van driver was lost. Her mother climbed aboard, calm as always, and pointed the way.

Adrienne told her, "Thanks, Mom, we can take it from here. We're getting too far away."

Sandra smiled. "No problem. I plan to walk home anyway."

She stepped off the van and disappeared down the road, walking strong and sure into the fog just like when Adrienne was a little girl.

By 2020, the world closed. COVID turned safety into stillness.

Isolation protected Sandra's lungs but punished her legs. She lay in bed in a fetal position due to acute paralysis in her knees.

The house shrank to a recliner, a bed, a window, and an Amazon Echo Show for pop-in video calls from family and friends.

Sandra was not perfect. She was loud, impulsive, and larger than life, but she was good.

Of all the adults who had broken things, she was the one who protected the children. She was often the only adult in the room.

She did not deserve the pain life gave her, but she carried it with grace. She could have exposed every wrong done to her, but she chose forgiveness instead.

Her home stayed open, a soft place to land. She defended her children with the strength of a soldier and the faith of a saint.

Near the end, Sandra's sister Beverly asked the question that always rises when love and faith meet loss. "God, why her?"

Adrienne could almost hear her mother answer, soft and certain.

"Why not me?"

Sandra was definitive. She and God would decide when it was her time. No doctors, no illness, no circumstance. Just God.

The morning of her transition was quiet. Sunlight spilled across the room, soft and golden, touching the corners first, then her face.

Sandra rested peacefully, her breath shallow but calm.

When the moment came, there was no fear, only release.

It was less like leaving and more like returning.

Her work was done.

The woman who had carried so much had finally been carried home.

And as for Barry, Sandra had always been his soul tie.

They had the kind of connection that lives beneath logic and beyond circumstance. It was rooted in shared history, in the years they survived together, in the wounds they gave and the forgiveness she offered without fanfare.

A soul tie does not ask permission; it lingers, it pulls, it reminds.

And for Barry, Sandra was the one presence he could never outrun, the one truth that refused to fade, no matter where life carried him or who stood beside him.

She sacrificed her career to stand beside him as a military wife, raised his children and his sister's child, poured herself into his family with a loyalty that outpaced his own, and forgave him long before he ever picked up the phone to say he was sorry.

They had formed a covenant, a promise spoken young but lived through decades of triumph and heartbreak, and she never let it fracture.

In Sandra's unmistakable style, she left one final message for Barry, her high school sweetheart.

"On this day, you will remember your first wife and celebrate your last wife."

Sandra passed away on May 21, 2024, Barry's third wife's birthday.

He would honor Sandra too, beyond death do them part.

As for her children, she taught them that faith was not the absence of struggle but the strength to walk through it.

In that truth, she never really left.

She had one final request for them. Go straight to the repast and turn it into a celebration.

Just like every house party, backyard gathering, and holiday she ever hosted, they brought Sandra's style to life one more time.

They called the DJ, served the food, wore the matching shirts, and opened the doors to the entire community.

They line danced, they laughed, they filled the room with her spirit, and she was the life of the party because it was her life they were celebrating.

Sandra gave her children more than guidance; she gave them a foundation so strong it still carried them long after life tried to break them.

Every lesson, every sacrifice, every moment of fierce love stayed rooted in their bones.

Her passing did not silence the house; it sanctified it.

The air shifted, softened, as if gratitude itself had settled into the walls. And in the days that followed, her children turned their grief into action, carrying her love forward the only way they knew how.

What began as a promise became a calling.

They created The Sandra Fund in their mother's honor, rooted in the work closest to her legacy. It champions organ donation, especially in communities of color where need is great and awareness is often low.

It stands as a bridge for those who are waiting, healing, and praying for another chance at life. It connects donors, recipients, and advocates through the same faith that carried Sandra through every storm.

The mission was clear.

Give others what Sandra gave her family; strength, hope, and the will to keep moving forward.

Every story shared, every life saved, every act of giving became a thread in the legacy she left behind.

The Sandra Fund is more than a tribute. It is living proof that love, once planted, never dies. It grows. It gives. It continues.

Sandra still visits Adrienne in her dreams.

Her voice from the stairs. The van on the road.

Her mother always walking ahead, showing the way home and then fading away like she did in the fog at the bottom of the hill in Germany.

Just like the Sarahbeth Taite song, *Mother's Daughter*, Adrienne stands on the shoulders of her mother's strength, walking the same road with reverence and prayer that her steps would honor the woman who came before her.

Sandra's eyes held a quiet holiness, her words a kind of prayer that steadied the broken and the lonely. Their bond ran deeper than blood, rooted in faith, love, and legacy.

In every way that mattered, Adrienne is her mother's daughter.

Now for Adrienne, the Parkway feels different. The drive is quieter, lighter in traffic but heavier in memory.

There are fewer stops to make, fewer doors waiting to open, yet every mile holds an echo of the life she once lived.

Every exit carries a story. She can still feel every summer on the Shore, every late-night diner run, every breath of salt air the moment she crosses the bridge.

People love to talk about Jersey. They always have something to say.

Jersey can take the jokes. It always has.

Because the truth is simple. The ones who clown it are usually the same ones who crave it.

They cannot admit their quiet obsession with the state,

because if they did, they would have to stop saying shit about Jersey.

# ACKNOWLEDGMENTS

My deepest thanks to every person who sat for an interview and trusted this project with their memories and their truth. Your voices shaped the backbone of this work.

To my **Mother, Sandra,** thank you for your Black Mom Magic.

To my **Father, Barry**, thank you for your honesty.

To my **Sister, Crystal**, thank you for your courage.

To my **Brothers, Barry Jr., Carlos, and Sonny** thank you for your support.

To my **Aunts**, thank you for your contributions and the pieces of history only you could give.

To my **Children, Kamilah, Makeda, and DeAngelus,** thank you for my inspiration.

A special thank you to my **Husband, Michael**, who believed this story was worth telling and encouraged me to speak my truth every step of the way.

To all my **Beta Readers**, thank you for your early reviews and honest feedback helped strengthen this story from the ground up.

To my **Fruit Bowl and Avenue family**, thank you for the love, the history, and the legacy that raised me. You are the community under every page.

To **Bailey West**, thank you for being an extraordinary writing coach and guide. Your insight, patience, and encouragement helped me find my voice and trust my words. You can find Bailey West's novels at **www.bailey-west.com**, on Amazon, and wherever books are sold.

# About the Author

Adrienne Michelle is an oral historian who captures the stories of ordinary people living extraordinary journeys. She listens with intention, gathers memories with care, and shapes experiences into narratives that honor truth, protect lineage, and preserve the histories that often go untold.

Her debut work, The One Son, is a deeply personal narrative exploring family, faith, and the choices that shape generations.

A New Jersey native and proud member of Delta Sigma Theta Sorority, Inc., Adrienne holds graduate degrees in African American History, Library Science, and Instructional Systems Development.

Adrienne is a strategic program leader and non-profit advocate. With more than 25 years of federal service, she leads teams, supports innovative learning systems, and develops programs that strengthen communities and expands opportunities.

As a co-founder for the **SANDRAFUND.org**, a nonprofit committed to advancing health equity and organ donation awareness. The Support & Awareness Network for Donors, Recipients, and Advocates (SANDRA) fund aspires to carry forward her mother's legacy, providing support and opportunities to those in need and promoting the values she held dear. It is more than just a fund; it is a celebration of her mother's spirit and an enduring commitment to her vision of a brighter, more equitable future.

Adrienne also curates the Adrienne Michelle Project, a purpose-driven collaboration built around three connected pathways: Growth, Storytelling, and Advocacy.

Through the Adrienne Michelle Project, she helps people reflect on their journeys, find meaning in their experiences, and turn those lessons into purposeful action. At the center of all her work is one simple truth: every life holds a story worth telling, and every story has the power to inspire change. You can join the journey at **AMICHELLEPROJECT.com.**

www.ingramcontent.com/pod-product-compliance
Lightning Source LLC
Chambersburg PA
CBHW032119090426
42743CB00007B/397